WILD ISLAND

Best Wishes
Peter Double
April 1996

Cover: Kestrel at La Rocque;
Overleaf: Wheatear at St. Ouen's

Wild Island

Jersey Nature Year

Peter Double

Illustrations by Nick Parlett

SEAFLOWER BOOKS

Published in 1996 by
SEAFLOWER BOOKS
16 1/2 New St. John's Road
St. Helier
Jersey

Seaflower Books is an imprint of Ex Libris Press, to whom all enquiries and correspondence should be addressed:

EX LIBRIS PRESS
1 The Shambles
Bradford on Avon
Wiltshire
BA15 1JS

Design and typesetting by Ex Libris Press

Cover printed by Shires Press, Trowbridge, Wiltshire

Printed and bound by Cromwell Press, Broughton Gifford, Wiltshire

ISBN 0 948578 77 7

CONTENTS

'A very large hedgehog stood by the dog's bowl devouring his leftovers.'
– see page 113

PREFACE

I've come to the conclusion that no matter how much we learn about the natural world during our life span, it remains only the tip of a very large iceberg and, because most of us do not have the ability to score maximum points in the 'Trivial Pursuits' of life, questions will always arise which remain unanswered.

As we progress through Jersey's nature calendar, or at least my view of it, there will be a few questions. There will be reference to the boundless pleasure nature has seen fit to bestow upon me over the years too but, by and large, this book is about Jersey. What I have recorded here and described, sometimes in detail, sometimes not, may be seen by anyone, given the right time of year, a love of the great outdoors and a good field guide.

From the naturalist's point of view, the Island is unique, not so much for its rare species, though Jersey is blessed with its fare share of those, but because it gives comparatively easy access to a variety of wild habitats.

The inter-tidal zone is rich in marine and bird life. Footpaths cut into the sides of three and four hundred foot cliffs on the north coast provide endless interest for the nature lover. There are heathland and woodland walks, ancient sand dunes and, on the west coast, a storm beach of majestic proportions. None of these delights is more than twenty minutes by car from any point in the Island.

Despite the modernisation of farming techniques, the Island's barn owl population is surprising healthy. Red squirrels hold their own in wooded areas because their grey cousins, so prolific on the mainland, were never introduced to the Islands.

There are bottle-nosed dolphins in our offshore waters. Their hunting grounds range from the Ecréhous, a tiny group of islands between Jersey's north-east coast and the French mainland, to a point west of Cape Finistère. This southerly group is sighted regularly around the Island and is one of only three communities in British waters.

The growth rate of bass is six times that of mainland fish and recently introduced oyster farms are thriving, thanks to the richness of our coastal waters.

Wild Island

The years vary in Jersey almost as much as the seasons and months. Drought, excessive rainfall, the loss of 52,000 trees in 1987 in a single night of hurricane force winds – all affect the diary of a naturalist – but the Island has experienced these natural events many times before and has recovered. It's fair to say that the only phenomenon 'wild' Jersey finds difficult to cope with is us – *homo sapiens.*

The pressures on this small and still beautiful Island are enormous. The resident population has increased from 50,000 to 84,000 in four decades.

We have paid and still are paying a forfeit for economic success and, unless we take great care, the pressures on our wild environment could result in eventual over-load. The Island's natural heritage is under constant siege and defending it has become a battle for the future. Lose the battle and I am convinced Jersey will lose its soul.

P.D.

La Rocco from sand dunes at St. Ouen's

JANUARY

I CLIMBED THE TIMBER STEPS up to L'Oeillière at La Pulente very much aware of 'festive joints.' From this high vantage point, the whole sweep of St. Ouen's Bay opens up into a great sickle of sand and surf. The bay faces west and, if one stands on the hard impacted sands of the beach, where, in high summer, the gutteral roar of racing cars bounces off the old German defences, it is said that there is nothing between you and Nova Scotia.

L'Oeillière is one of the few places where the true size and shape of La Pinacle rock at the northern-most tip of the bay may be seen. It climbs two hundred feet out of the sea like an enormous standing stone. In its shadow, on the rabbit-clipped grasses of the landward side, there was once an Iron Age village. The great rock has been witness to skirmish and worship over the centuries and still has a strange atmosphere about it even in summer when gorse pods snap and a carpet of thrift and sea campion brightens the cliff.

On the headland the gorse is in bloom despite strong winds – a sure sign that the beginning of this New Year is unseasonably mild. As I stood there enjoying the half-tide view I watched a kestrel leaning into the strong breeze. He appeared to be fairly open-minded about his diet. The terrain below him was perfect for small rodents but it was a greenfinch that caught his eye. I watched the convolutions of the chase until both birds disappeared out across Petit Port bay, heading in the general direction of La Corbière lighthouse.

From L'Oeillière I retraced my steps and headed north to the sand dunes at Les Blanches Banques, determined to shake out the last of the 'festive fuzz.' The place has changed little since Neolithic times – ancient sand dunes, timeless standing stones, age-old plants and, to add a sense of moment to the scene, there was a party of ravens tumbling in the wind at the lip of the eastern escarpment. With a little imagination you might still hear the sounds of flint-napping and the rattle of limpet shells being tossed into some midden above the dull roar of pounding surf and whispering marram grass. Only the sharp-edged German bunkers

Standing Stone,
Les Blanches Banques

tucked strategically into the sides of the dunes below La Moye golf course gave the 'time travel' game away.

There are over four hundred species of plants among the dunes and along the bay behind the sea defences. Some are so tiny that even on hands and knees they are hard to find. But that's a summer-time pursuit to be enjoyed with skylark song, gentle breezes and bee talk.

Sunshine, rainbows, showers and colder. Only the temperature insists it's not April. There's no doubt January is a month for birds because deep in the wood very little stirs and yet, in the air, in hedgerows, meadows and on the seashore there is constant activity.

In my parish, St. Clement, mallard are feeding in the stubble of a maize field. They are working shoulder to shoulder with a large flock of feral pigeons which commutes daily from its St. Helier roost. Beyond the maize field, over a bramble hedge, thickened blackthorn and the gaunt remains of dead elms, a mixture of little egrets and grey herons are sheltering. They stand on their own reflections beneath willow and oak in the flooded corner of a marshy meadow. The birds spend their time there during spring tides when their offshore roosts are awash or if gales force them to find shelter inland.

Nick Parlett and I decided to plan an Island wide bird watch while there was so much activity. About sixty-five species seemed like a reasonable target, especially if the tides and weather conditions were right. The Island is full of bird life at the moment with wintering migrants adding their names to the resident list. The final tally should be quite impressive even for a small lump of granite, nine by five miles, in the middle of winter! Conditions don't look too good at the moment though. There's rain sweeping in from the south-west in thick grey columns bringing poor visibility with it.

Kestrel

Lots of floodwater to encourage waders and wildfowl. There are extra pools, puddles and ponds everywhere at the moment thanks to copious amounts of rain and, because it has been a wet winter, it should be some time before they melt into the ground. For some reason they seem especially attractive to our wintering black-headed gulls. Raucous they may be but, in my opinion, in shape and form they are the most beautiful of all the family *Larus* and no, I haven't forgotten the kittiwake !

Of Birds, Ticks and Calvados

The planned Island tour, with copious amounts of bird-watching on the way, began at about 9.30 am on a cold but sun-blessed morning. Not a particularly early start, quite civilised in fact, but at this time of year sunrise comes late and birds feed pretty much throughout the day. Birds have no time for mid-day siestas in winter.

The wind was from the north so the bird watch, which began on the east coast, started in fairly calm conditions. The tide had been dropping for a couple of hours and a low water moonscape of rocky heads, stretching away into the distance, was slowly emerging from the sea.

The tide on this coast drops a good mile and a half on a spring. It's a place of granite outcrops, weed-shaded pools and sand and shingle banks running like ice leads through a complicated system of gullies and gutters. It is not a place for the unwary. Sometimes the rising tide gives ample warning, moving noisily through the rocky channels, encircling reefs and filling gullies with the fast-flowing surge of a tidal river. At other times it will move in with a covert stealth, submerging familiar landmarks as it goes. Even the most experienced low water fishermen can be caught out on this coast.

To us the scene may be one of desolation, but to the thousands of birds who winter on the east coast it provides a rich source of food and a secure roost at a time when their summer quarters are in the grip of sub-zero temperatures.

In the first fifteen minutes we logged twenty species including red-breasted merganser, great crested grebe and a couple of deliciously delicate greenshanks. When they came in from the off-shore rocks the greenshanks landed short of the barely uncovered sand in a small rocky bay. They sat on the sea, breasting the wavelets like a pair of phalaropes. I know they like to wade in quite deep pools, but to see them afloat was delightful.

There were at least a couple of hundred dark-bellied Brent geese muttering noisily among the shallow pools created by the ebbing tide. Over the last twenty years or so they have become a major ingredient in the enjoyment of Jersey's foreshore. They arrive from their Siberian breeding grounds over a period of several weeks in autumn and their untidy chevrons are harbingers of winter.

Not much bigger than a mallard, these smallest of geese keep us company until the last stragglers leave in spring. In the late 1980s Brent goose arrivals in Jersey increased from around eight hundred to a remarkable fifteen hundred. The reason given for the increase was fascinating and underlines how ecological change on another continent can affect this small island of ours.

At their breeding grounds, Brent geese are susceptible to predation by Arctic foxes. The increase in Brents arriving in Jersey corresponded with a massive lemming population explosion at the birds' summer breeding quarters. The Arctic foxes turned to a diet of lemmings instead of goslings, resulting in a far higher survival rate. Jersey numbers increased accordingly.

We moved inland from the coast to Le Prés Manor, a place of ancient farm buildings and low-lying marshy meadows. A brook runs through the rough farmland and, given sufficient rainfall, it overflows into the fields in winter. The meadows are peppered with tufts of soft rush. Among the tall grasses, glazed with plashes of flood water, we caught occasional glimpses of moorhen, teal, and shoveller duck. No sign of snipe. They *are* there of course, but unless they move, their plumage, streaked with the yellows, browns and buff of winter, makes them impossible to see, even with good binoculars and an abundance of patience.

A single pink-footed goose provided an unexpected bonus. We listed it, despite having misgivings about its qualifications, and then headed for Waterworks Valley where we hoped we would hear, if not see, jays and great spotted woodpecker.

In summer, this valley of reservoirs and chuckling streams is lush with wild flowers. The sweet chestnut, sycamore, and oak climbing the steep slopes are leaf-clad and filled with bird song. Hover-flies hover and bumble bees search the ivy among the narrow columns of sunlight penetrating the upper canopy. In January, there's just the occasional contact call from dunnock and wren and the sound of running water. Bare branches give the sun unhindered access to the valley floor and there is a silence that can only mean winter.

The valley gave us some small birds – long-tailed tit, chiffchaff and bullfinch; as we'd hoped, the raucous call of a jay split the stillness and was rapidly followed by the briefest flash of pale blue wing bars and a fast disappearing, snowy white rump.

We were glad to leave the valley, albeit woodpeckerless. We would return there at a better time of year. Meanwhile the steep winding road led us up into the sunlight and the bare flat fields of the northern parishes. At Plémont we found fulmar, stiff-winged and barrel-shaped, coarsing the cliffs beneath us. Offshore there was a raft of some two hundred birds riding the swells. An exciting prospect for the breeding season.

Fulmar Petrel

Fulmar numbers have built up considerably over the last two decades, much to the delight of Island birdwatchers and as predicted in the book *Birds of the Channel Islands.* The book was written by the late Roderick Dobson and published in 1952. His notes on the fulmar petrel state, 'An occasional wanderer to the Channel Islands. It is generally recognised by ornithologists that the breeding range of the fulmar is spreading southwards very gradually. *I prophesy that the next generation will see a few pairs breeding in the Islands.'* How right he was. Today, on the north-western and northern coasts of Jersey, these oceanic masters of flight are quite a common sight all year round.

Plémont, near the north-western tip of the Island, is always a good place to be. It gives access to the north coast cliff walks, and provides by far the finest views of the other Channel Islands. On this occasion the clarity was stunning. Alderney, thirty-two miles away, was almost touchable. Beside it, a white insubstantial finger jutted out of the sea. Could it possibly be a mirage of the formidable Casquets lighthouse reef ?

Our final stop on this New Year tour was Jersey's largest area of fresh water, St. Ouen's Pond. It's on the Island's west coast and was, at one time, an inlet set into the dunes. Now it is a place of phragmites reed beds, cetti's warblers and fat, double-figure carp.

It also provides a terrific roosting place for wildfowl and gulls and, if you are lucky, possibly a hunting marsh harrier, peregrine falcon or merlin.

On this day the pond provided none of these species. What it did bless us with, as we

Bittern, St. Ouen's Pond

sipped the remains of the Christmas calvados from an ever more hollow sounding hip flask, was a bittern. A first for both of us and a great new tick for the list.

The bird lifted from its hiding place and gave us a magnificent fly-past before dipping down once again into the shelter of the straw-coloured reed beds. We made notes, shook hands, grinned all over our faces and added bittern to the list, which, on the final tally, had reached a very satisfying sixty-eight species. The time was 3.15 p.m.

For those readers who find lists interesting or who might, perhaps, wish to compare notes, the species sighted are listed below under the areas in which they were actually seen:

LA ROCQUE HARBOUR
Cormorant, Grey Heron, Greenshank, Redshank, Grey Plover, Ring Plover, Brent Goose, Dunlin, Sanderling, Turnstone, Red-breasted Merganser, Great-crested Grebe, Rock Pipit, Pied Wagtail, Oyster-catcher, Great Black-backed Gull, Golden Plover, Little Egret;

LE PRES MANOR, GROUVILLE
Teal, Mallard, Shoveller Duck, Moorhen, Coot, Carrion Crow, Magpie, Chaffinch, Blackbird, Mute Swan, Pink-footed Goose, Starling, Herring Gull, Curlew, Chiffchaff, Collared Dove;

SAMARES MANOR
Blue Tit, Great Tit, Redwing, Fieldfare, Mistle-thrush, Song Thrush, Robin, Lapwing, House Sparrow, Dunnock, Wood Pigeon, Wren, Snipe, Black-headed Gull;

WATERWORKS VALLEY
Jay, Tufted duck, Feral pigeon, Bullfinch, Goldfinch, Long-tailed tit, Tree creeper, Blackcap;

PLEMONT
Fulmar, Stonechat, Raven;

ST. OUEN'S POND
Meadow pipit, European pochard, Stock dove, Gadwall, Cetti's warbler, Water rail, Shag, Greenfinch, Bittern.

The Brer Facts

It's a good thing rabbits don't hibernate otherwise January would be totally bereft of mammals, ones that are easy to see that is. There are signs of course. Neat little twin-toothed chisel cuts on the caps of old fungi and kestrel pellets containing mouse and vole fur. But it is nice to see the flash of a scut amongst the gorse bushes on the opposite hill and to know that the Island's rabbit population is surviving, if not thriving.

Before the arrival of myxomatosis it was thought that there were between sixty and one hundred million rabbits in Britain. In September 1953 the disease was introduced to the mainland and within three years had wiped out 99% of the population. It apparently took some time to reach the Channel Islands because it was not until 1958/59 that rabbits there began dying in large numbers. There is still myxomatosis in Jersey but its effects seem to have lessened over the last few years. A high percentage of rabbits actually recover from the disease now or would if they manage to avoid the attention of predators. Jersey has no foxes but cats, crows, ravens and escaped polecats and ferrets all provide the rabbit with a reason to keep open a wary eye.

It's easy to take rabbits for granted. They're simply there. They've *always* been there. But when I delved into my own knowledge of *Oryctolagus cuniculus*, not surprisingly, I discovered I knew very little. Did you know, for example, that they are not native to Britain? They came from the Iberian Peninsula – Spain and Portugal.

My borrowed text book informed me that there is some doubt as to when they were introduced to Britain but, as there is no mention of them, or warrens, in the Domesday Book, it must have been after 1066 and all that.

They may have been brought to England by monks accompanying Knights returning from the Crusades and kept in warrens as a food source. I wonder which monk allowed a couple to escape? Oops! There goes lunch and nine hundred years later we have fifty million.

Creemation

I'm all for cutting fuel bills in winter and in order to 'stay loose' I prefer to do it with a couple of steel wedges and my trusty ten pound sledge hammer. Because of a couple of hurricanes, Dutch Elm disease and, occasionally, old age, the Island has lost an estimated 250,000 mature trees since the war. It was while swinging the trusty sledge that I experienced the most bizarre moment in my wood-cutting life.

My home overlooks Samarès Manor. The manor has the finest herb gardens in Britain, a beautiful, circular granite pigeon house called a *colombier*, an extraordinary collection of camellias and some fine trees. One of the trees, a beech, had been cut down for safety reasons and I had laid claim to a rather large piece of its trunk.

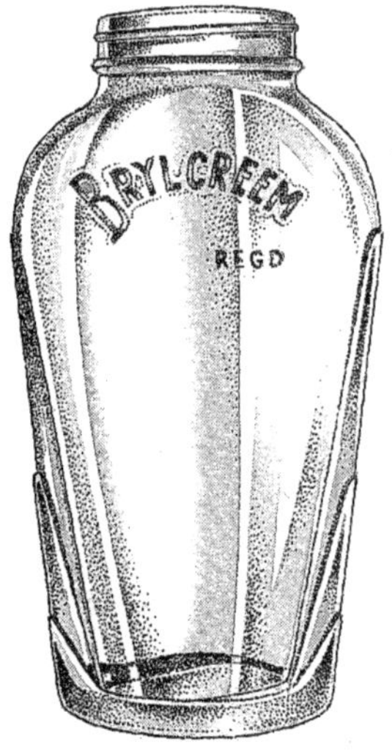

The trunk was sliced into rounds measuring about four feet across and had been stacked loosely, one on top of the other, to dry out. Several of the rounds had a large split in the centre running vertically through the trunk. At their widest point the splits were about five or six inches across, tapering to nothing at the outer extremities. The split in each slice of trunk was filled with a sort of loamy detritus, probably the result of a gradual build-up from at least a hundred autumns.

For about an hour the wood pile grew, so did the ache in my back and the dog was getting bored. I split the last slice of beech like a birthday cake, working my way round it segment by segment. About a third had gone when the hammer swung, hit the wedge with a satisfying thud; following the thud I distinctly heard a 'clink.' Peering over the slab of wood I saw a very dirty, but complete, glass bottle lying on the concrete. The bottle had come from the loam and the proof lay in the perfect impression of its shape pressed into dark mould. I gave it a good wash in a nearby pond and discovered it was a Brylcreem jar registration No 21, bottle No 882.

I have two books on trees. One is of the 'and Europe' variety and the other is the 'of the World' type. Neither told me the life expectancy of a beech tree. I didn't count the rings because this particular chain saw didn't leave them very clear and, being a bit of a nature novice, I'm never quite sure which are the rings and which are the bits in between.

So how did a sixty year old Brylcreem bottle get into the middle of a mature beech tree? Did the tree grow and lift the jar with it in the fork? Did some disgruntled suitor chuck it over his shoulder when the smooth, shiny look of his mop failed to attract the apple of his eye ? Or did some genetically advanced squirrel keep his nuts in it ? I'll leave your imagination to contemplate the possibilities, dear reader.

St. Ouen's Pond in winter

FEBRUARY

Roof-nesting herring gulls

FEBRUARY IS PROBABLY JERSEY'S most unpredictable time of year. Over a period of twenty-five years, in the very same month, I've filmed honey bees enjoying the nectar from snowdrops and stood on ice flows in St. Aubin's Bay when the sea has frozen. I can only recommend that, if February offers a suggestion of Spring, take it, enjoy it, then expect the worst. In terms of weather, it's a month not to be trusted.

Inland, the fields are saturated with rain water, much to the delight of flocks of opportunistic herring gulls. The birds stride the fallow fields in a most orderly fashion, gleaning earthworms and larvae washed out of the ground by persistent rain. Their diet is totally uninhibited and, on this small Island, they have become very wise. The hunt for earth worms is a regular occupation at this time of year.

The majority of Jersey's herring gull population still uses the steep cliffs of the south-west and northern coasts to breed but, following the trend throughout Britain, more and more Island birds are finding town and country roof-tops useful alternatives.

From their roosts and nest sites on the roofs of St. Helier, the birds have learned about cafés, fish and chip shops and restaurants *and* about the contents of the black plastic bags that appear, ready for collection, late at night. In summer, their early morning cries echo through the town as they skirmish over a carelessly tied bag and feed on its spilled contents.

Later in the year some will join the black-headed gulls, spiralling up on the thermals to feed on flying ants lifted by warm air and they can be seen at any time gaining entry to cockles and crabs by letting them fall fifty or sixty feet onto rocky seashore outcrops. They are also avid followers of the plough and enjoy the cranefly harvest in autumn.

On reflection, I doubt whether a single Jersey bird has ever earned the name 'herring' gull just because of its diet.

I once read in the *Scottish Ornithologist*, an account of a herring gull whose casual attitude to diet was its undoing. Heavy and prolonged rain had caused flooding and one casualty of the deluge was a mole. The poor beast lay among the puddles of a country lane covered in mud. A herring gull discovered the body and, after a couple of tentative prods, swallowed the mole whole and continued its aerial search for flood victims.

Unfortunately for the gull, the mole was not dead. The body heat from the herring gull must have had a reviving effect because the mole simple burrowed its way out of the bird's neck and both animals were killed in the ensuing crash.

Mole

Ground-hugging greenhouses

Greenhouse Effect

During the first few days of February the earliest Jersey Royal potatoes are planted on the southern-facing cotîls. These tiny fields, clinging to steep hillsides, are prepared by cutting the furrows with a plough shear winched up the field via the versatile ingenuity of Massey Ferguson, John Brown and a few with more ancient manufacturers' names.

The potatoes are planted by hand and immediately disappear under a sheet of cold, grey, plastic before this faithless month can touch the tender root crop with icy fingers.

By month's end, the southern fields will be in the grip of what appears to be a new Ice Age. These sheets of plastic, perforated with thousands of holes to allow excess heat out, protect the early crop from frost and generate warmth to encourage growth.

How this endless coat of rippling polythene affects wildlife has not been properly assessed. Its effect on me is to prolong the feeling of winter. But as the weather softens and the growers put their trust in March, these ground-hugging greenhouses begin to disappear and the great agricultural thaw sets in.

The land becomes green again, the sun gathers warmth and farmers gain confidence.

Fishing Limits

Once upon time, when the Island was a part of continental Europe, several rivers, including the Seine, flowed across a great plain separating Brittany from the huge granite outcrop which later would become Jersey. The course of one of these rivers – and it would be nice to think it *was* the Seine – passed within a mile and a half of Bouley Bay harbour on the north coast. The old river bed shows up on ships' echo sounders like a steep canyon cut deep into the seabed and is now haunted by conger eels and shoals of pout whiting instead of fresh-run salmon, pike and carp.

That's the closest Jersey ever came to having its very own river but there is enough fresh water to provide anglers with a chance to relax and enjoy a little therapy. Several species of fish have been introduced to the Island's reservoirs over the years, including roach, tench, bream and perch and there's a strong head of locally bred brown and rainbow trout too. Wild carp, rudd and common eels are probably the only species caught by anglers that are indigenous to the Island.

There was a time when Jersey's coarse fishing closed season began in February, a month earlier than the dates set by mainland Britain. Presumably it was because our milder climate was thought to induce fish to breed earlier but, in recent years, club anglers have decided to conform with the mainland closed season dates – March 14th to June 16th. Apparently, at least where carp are concerned, it's a time clock rather than a thermometer that sets them on the road to procreation. Frantic activity well after the opening of the local season presumably convinced anglers that their dates were a little premature.

Carp are plentiful in the Island's larger stretches of fresh water and can often be seen around the margins of Val de la Mare and the old German reservoir near St. Catherine's on hot summer days, basking lazily on the surface. There are some huge fish amongst them. Specimens of up to twenty pounds have been taken on rod and line and other, great sovereign-coated giants, have been sighted with estimated weights of well over the thirty pound mark. So, with the coarse angler's habitat out of bounds for three months and the tackle is tackle undergoing repairs and maintenance, the sea is where the angler's serious interest lies in February. It's not a month for numbers of fish, but at night around breakwaters and rocky promontories, big conger and pollack often turn up. There are some large bass too, foraging in the undertows of wave-pounded beaches and among the gullies just beyond the low tide surf.

Catching these big winter fish really is a waiting game. They test the patience, hardiness and the knowledge of anglers and, occasionally, the rewards justify the discomfort of cold winds, damp feet and frozen fingers. To see a twelve pound bass rolling in the surf, gleaming in the flickering light of a torch, and to watch the foaming lip of tide finally leave it stranded ashore is, for an angler, the culmination of years of optimism, fruitless nights and pipe dreams.

Bass chasing sand-eels

Looking back through angling reports I've written for various publications over the past thirty years, rays take up a great deal of February column space. The Island holds the British shore-caught undulate ray record, a fish of 21lbs.4ozs., taken from St. Catherine's breakwater. Dozens of hefty fish are landed from this granite pier but always in February, early March and in late autumn. It's almost as if the Island's north-eastern tip is a migration path. The pattern of reports are far too regular to be coincidental.

In my youth I worked a drawnet with a few friends, mostly in Ouaisné Bay. It was a simple, well tried method of catching fish. A fifty metre net, eight feet deep, with floats at the head and weights at the foot. The net was towed out by a small dinghy in a great semicircle while two fishermen held the end, attached to a pole. Steady rowing pulled the net off the stern until the semi-circle was completed and the boat grated ashore.

As an angler and naturalist, what fascinated me was the variety of species taken when the net was hauled ashore. In the moonlight, mullet could be seen leaping over the outer rim of the net and it was very rare that any were landed. All the flat fish were represented however – plaice, tiny sole, turbot, brill and flounder and even small true whiting, quite a rarity in local waters. Cuttlefish, with their ink glands, blackened the fish box. Green crabs managed to tangle the net with their usual dexterity, ably assisted by small spider crabs. All these species were from water no more than six feet deep.

And then there were the rays. I actually listed them in my diary – thornback, undulate, blonde, small-eyed and one or two others that were difficult to identify by torch light. None of the rays were more than side plate size and all were, needless to say, returned to the water.

The experience suggested that Jersey's inshore waters could be the breeding ground for a variety of ray species and that a moonlit drawnetting session could possibly have revealed where the nursery grounds were.

Yellow is the Colour ...

Just a small dent in February and early morning fog softens the brittle fingers of winter trees. Even without drawing the bedroom curtains the silence gives the weather away. The house feels as though it's wrapped in cotton wool and the dull roar of the Heathrow 'red eye' has yet to announce its departure. Then the light strengthens, the fog retreats and suddenly the sun breaks through. Avenues of intensely blue sky open between the clouds and announce that one of February's more gentle moods is in progress.

I decided to take a walk. The light and visibility were perfect and seemed to overemphasise the colours of a mixed flock of chaffinch and redwings in the hawthorns lining the meadow.

After almost two weeks of heavy rain, low grey skies and short days, a spell of sun seemed to make the simplest things brighter and more noticeable. The combination of yellow ochre lichen, the pink glow of local granite and paint splashes of bright green pennywort leaves, tucked into the crevices, made an everyday wall appear quite stunning.

I discovered the height of optimism in the form of a gentleman toad paddling the (so far) deserted waters of a local breeding pond. It seemed the rest of the toad population set about as much store in the reliability of February as me. I suspect it will be some days yet before they get the urge to test the water with a webbed toe and join this 'early bird'.

In Mont Ubé woods where, later in the year, violets grow in great numbers, I found lesser celandine – two small splashes of bright shiny yellow nestling among the ivy leaves carpeting the woodland floor. Another couple of weeks and they will compete in colour and numbers with the wayward clumps of daffodils, their spikes already showing strongly through the leaf mould. In many cases the daffodils are hybrids which were once part of crops grown in the fields at the top of the escarpment. This extra early spring treat occurs all over the Island where cultured flowers have been grown. Woodlands, hedgerows and fields which have lain fallow for years, all produce their quota of colour and only the horticulturist might, perhaps, realise just how many varieties there are amongst the wild daffodils.

Celandine

My walk was accompanied by bird song too. The bold notes of a song thrush laying claim to his patch struck me as just a little early considering the date, but he was ably supported by robin, dunnock and wren. I concluded that they probably knew something I didn't. There was no wind on the wooded slopes and it gave the bird song a kind of unimpeded clarity normally only heard in stereo on the radio.

The 'radio' observation got me thinking about media sound and natural history. It's strange the odd thoughts that pass through the almost sub-conscious mind when enjoying a walk on the wild side. Why is it that when radio and television sound effects departments want to give the impression that it's night time and there could be something rather nasty about, they use the sound of a male peacock on heat? Their other favourites seem to be buzzard and great northern diver. I think it's about time all three species appeared in the end credits.

The St. Aubin's 'Stuka'

Mid-February is still very much a bird time of year in Jersey and my observations of this *ultimate* winter month feature some very special moments. The time I began counting a large flock of black-backed gulls on the windswept sands of St. Ouen's beach is a good example. I suddenly realised that the small group of black and white birds beyond them were avocets, not oyster-catchers. Such a rare treat for the Island and a perfect example of what can so easily be missed, especially when fingers are frozen and, because of their familiarity, roosting gulls are only given a cursory glance.

Wild Island

My finest February moment happened one morning when I had just parked my car in the boat-filled, duck-friendly village of St. Aubin's, on the western side of the bay of the same name. The village used to be one of those that survived the winter by battening down the hatches, lowering the metabolic rate of the restaurant work force and hibernating until 'Holiday Britain' rediscovered it in early June. These days it's just as delightful but with a parking problem, due largely, I suspect, to the fact that it *is* delightful. St. Aubin's bustles these days, all year round.

Anyway, I got out of the car, glanced up at a bunch of herring gulls enjoying an early morning argument on a helpful south-easterly wind and noticed this 'full stop' hanging about a hundred feet above them. The 'full stop' suddenly fell into a fast, steep dive, cut through the gulls, jinxed neatly between the mastheads in the harbour and nipped over the eastern arm of the harbour wall. It was a display of flying skill by a supreme master.

There was complete uproar among the mixed waders feeding on the tide line on the far side of the pier. This St. Aubin's 'Stuka' was up and circling the panicking curlews, dunlin, redshanks and oyster-catchers well before they had time to express their inadequate point of view.

It was, of course, a peregrine falcon just letting the local bird population know she was around. The whole exercise seemed to have been carried out just for the sheer hell of it and I stood stock-still in awe and admiration.

Why I should delight in the privilege of seeing a peregrine falcon I'm not sure. I feel I know them personally, thanks to the writings

The supreme master

of Henry Williamson, and yet just a half dozen glimpses in a lifetime is all I've had and it has been a great thrill every time.

There were peregrines breeding on all four major Channel Islands at one time but not any more, although with sightings becoming much more frequent over the last decade one can always live in hope, I suppose.

Shell Shock

The family 'Double' has acquired a tortoise. Yes it *is* the wrong time of year, at least I think it is, and yes, I agree it is not part of the *natural* sequence of events anticipated in this journal but such was the impact of this infant reptile on family life that some record of its onslaught on our otherwise steady routine should be duly noted.

What I knew about tortoises when 'Linford' joined the household could be written on the toenail of a short-tailed shrew. Lynford, four inches by four inches of disruptive influence from the moment he arrived, joined a hamster, an assortment of tropical fish, three cats, a golden retriever, two budgerigars, a multitude of large house spiders, and some house mice who enjoy living 'on the edge.' Compared to Linford the whole lot combined barely rippled the surface of our comparatively harmonious family bliss.

To pay a great deal of cash for a huge amount of worry is pretty illogical. Pets are supposed to be fun! I 'm never sure whether spending hours upside down in a bowl of water in his heated aquarium is fun for Linford but it's positively nail-biting for me!

It's not as if Linford is entertaining; I'd have more fun watching a stalactite grow a foot – in inches that is! Taking responsibility for a diminutive reptile that sleeps for several days at a time and enjoys pretending to be dead, wears out worry beads, dissolves fingernails and makes the dog hide under the bed – I think I'd rather try and sort out the differences between the plants in the carrot family than be responsible for the well-being of a tortoise!

Crow Time

The early February fog is persisting and the temperature today is a very unseasonable 13° C. From my den window I can see four or five hundred starlings feeding in the meadow. At one point they rose *en masse*, circled the field and, when they landed, the group expanded in a perfect circle outwards. I've not seen them do this before but it seems a perfect way to cover the ground thoroughly and without the usual arguments.

Carrion crows are beginning their oak-top meetings. I can see at least fifty birds congregating in a tree along the avenue leading to the rear of Samarès Manor as I write. These 'parliaments' are noisy affairs with birds drawn into serious discussion from miles around. There are occasional fights when tempers fray and discussion gets a little out of hand. A couple of birds lock together in battle, tumble through the branches and, just when you think they will part and avoid the ground, they thump right into it and then fly back into the meeting with no apparent harm done. I'm sure these incredibly raucous gatherings sort out who will be mating with whom in a week or two's time.

A prodigious feast

Weed Feed

At La Rocque, a black redstart is feeding on a hatch of fly. A little sun on the great piles of *vraic*, accumulated following a procession of south-westerly gales, has generated heat within the heaped mixture of oarweed, bladder and serrated *vraic*. The dark, pungent weed, piled high against the sea wall, has set the area abuzz. The black redstart, a winter visitor, is joined by rock pipits, pied wagtails and starlings. The larvae beneath the weed and the flies over it provide a prodigious feast.

There's quite a big tide and through the binoculars the inshore rocks are crowded with thousands of waders. The order of roost appears to be a simple one. If you are a small bird – purple sandpiper, dunlin or little stint – you only need a small ledge. I think that's the standard arrangement for off-shore rock accommodation among the waders. Small birds at the base of the rocks and a steady progression in size – plovers, godwits, curlews and even little egrets higher up. Not so much a pecking order, rather a perching order.

If the weather makes the lower ledges untenable it's not unusual to find the small waders comfortably settled on ploughed fields which, in Jersey, are never far from the sea.

In the settled waters of the harbour and sheltered bays close by about three hundred Brent geese mutter the high tide away and, off-shore, a raft of some thirty red-breasted mergansers ride the swells. The males look beautiful even in the dim, grey morning.

A good example of just how treacherous February can be for wildlife is the sad report I received this morning of a hedgehog road death. At least with a cold February they know where they stand, or sleep! Snug under a pile of leaves in some quiet wood is where they should be at this time of year, not being led astray by confused bumblebees and song thrushes.

MARCH

MY EARLIEST MEMORIES OF SEASONAL changes came, not from first-hand experiences of snow-drifts, showers, suntans and burning leaves, but from classroom posters. They described the seasons in a neat and precise format easily understood by a five-year-old who had brought his sandwiches to school in a gas-mask case and was learning to count using small brown and white cowrie shells on an ink-stained desk.

March, as far as those colourfully detailed illustrations were concerned, was the beginning of spring and that, as they say, was good enough for me. March winds, April showers and May bugs, flowers, poles and flies are all 'carved in stone' in my childhood memory and remain there still. Come to think of it, it was not just school posters that taught me how to categorise the seasons. My Christmas *Rupert Annual* managed it quite well too.

Later, however, I learned that the early days of any month always seemed to look suspiciously like the late days of the one before and the transition from season to season was a subtle period of blending rather than the clear dividing lines so beloved by cartographers, cartoonists and primary school posters.

Still in that far distant classroom, window ledge bulbs encased in bakelite pots and planted in what seemed like light years ago to a five-year-old, suddenly stood tall beside bowls filled with frog spawn. Those 'ecosystems' in jars and pots were proof enough that there was a metamorphosis taking place. Spring had arrived and there was a decidedly *different* feel to the air.

Masterful March

March, in the year I wrote this journal, roared in like the lion it can so often appear to be. Tall, blue-grey clouds, with heads like great anvils, advanced from the west-north-west, bearing thunder in their bellies and a thick swathe of hail at their skirts. There was an advanced guard – a buffeting, determined wind that rattled the blackthorns and drove gulls before it at incredible speed. Then the hail arrived in an almost horizontal sheet, bouncing off the car in the most spectacular manner. Suddenly it would stop, as if cut off by a switch. The sun crashed onto the scene and, as the hail storm chased away eastwards, a great rainbow stretched, with perfect clarity, from the broken teeth of the Minquiers reef to the very centre of St. Helier.

That's the advantage of living on an island with wonderfully high viewing platforms. Mine was Noirmont Point, where the passenger ferries pass beneath your feet and the views are not restricted by the canyons of a city. Such vantage points are wonderful places when the weather is being majestically dramatic. March weather certainly has its moments.

Hail-storm attacking Noirmont Point

Wild Island

I was right about the daffodils. They really are giving the celandines a run for their money. The celandines, with their burnished petals and deep green foliage, are at that hesitant stage, half-opened but not quite certain whether they should be so. The daffodils have no such misgivings. Bright yellow heads are appearing in hedgerows, banks, lanes and woodland and I've no doubt we will have the pleasure of their company for many weeks to come.

Bee Lines in Yellow

There's a veritable cloud of bees around the nearby hives and it's very early in the month. I traced the source of all the excitement to a huge camellia in full bloom. The flowers were a delicate pink and the heads, single rather than multi-petalled, were so numerous they almost hid the evergreen leaves which had carried their buds for months. The bees were emerging like bright yellow 'Dusty Millers' and as soon as one worker headed for home, another dived into the flower. Worker bees seem to lead a thankless existence. Team effort is all very well but it's all toil, dawn till dusk every day, and the lifespan of a worker is only about three weeks. Nature can be a hard task master, that's for sure.

March insisted on representing those childhood posters to the letter – intermittent hail, squalls and very large holes in the water. All the scene lacked was the traditional man hanging on to his hat while clinging to an inverted umbrella.

Crossing the Great Divide

I rolled, pitched and juddered my way to France for a few days early in the month; I've made the trip several dozen times and on each occasion I've wondered how we, as an island community, manage to enjoy the company of small summer migrant birds considering the very wide obstacle between us and the French coast. A half-ounce willow warbler, facing a flight that took our vessel three hours, must find the challenge somewhat daunting, if they think about it at all that is. Imagine the supreme confidence of the bird. From sea level, Jersey is not visible from any point on the coast of Brittany and yet, in spring, these tiny light-weights set off over a waste of water, the mood of which can change, literally, by the minute.

Once again nature is a hard task master because only the very strongest of the species, male and female, complete the journey and, at the end of a successful breeding season, both adults and newly fledged youngsters have to face the challenge, *en famille.*

It was a bit early for warblers to make the crossing but my business took me a kilometre north of the medieval town of Dinan where the River Rance was in full flow and the colour of strong tea. The banks were thick with butterbur, a kingfisher sat patiently above a small backwater eddy and blackthorn, broom and primroses were in bloom among the rocky buttresses above the river. Perhaps *this* was the river that ran close to Jersey before the salt-laden Atlantic claimed the lowlands and created islands where before there were none.

The trip back from La Belle France was, if anything, worse than the outward journey. There was a glimpse of razorbills flying low over steep, wind-blown waves, a solitary fulmar passed my salt-stained window, treating the weather with total nonchalance, and I looked in vain for an early gannet or two.

For the naturalist, a day trip to St. Malo or Granville during late spring and summer is always interesting. Given the right weather conditions, bird sightings are good. In Dinard black redstarts nest in the old town and on the steep, cliff-top walls of Granville, common redstarts can be seen regularly; I suspect they nest in the massive walls every year.

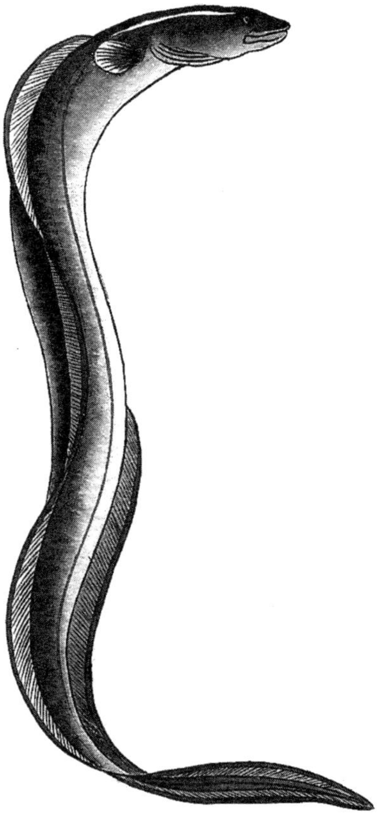

Eels on the Move

Several fine conger eels have been taken by anglers from the most unlikely places around Jersey this month. It's the middle of March and these eels, none of which were under thirty pounds and one almost fifty, were taken, not from rough reefy ground, as one might expect, but from areas where the sea bed is predominantly sand.

Could it be that fish of this size are preparing to migrate? It has been established that mature fish make a journey of several thousand miles to a point between Gibraltar and the Azores to spawn. Their destination is an area in the Atlantic where the water is between three and four thousand metres deep.

Even in an Island whose reputation for conger eel fishing is recorded in the Domesday Book, the natural history of the species is, to say the least, a bit sketchy. For example, we have not established at what stage conger eels become sexually mature, and it's a fact that no mature and sexually ripe congers have ever been caught. This could mean that they breed on the way down to the Azores or when they get there. It can't even be said for certain whether they mature by weight or by age but trends do show periods, some lasting several years, when large conger become less prolific in Jersey's coastal waters.

Wild Island

I find it fascinating to think that there is as much happening in the sea as on land at this time of year. The thought of thousands upon thousands of very large conger eels, many from the Jersey coast, streaming down instinctively towards their traditional midsummer breeding grounds off the African continent, is dramatic in the extreme.

Conger eels, like their freshwater brethren, do not return from this long journey south. The larvae resulting from this massive coming together of eels, is carried north-easterly with the current, eventually to drift into the comparatively shallow waters off the coasts of northern Europe, when the whole cycle begins again.

Fragile Frogs

Jersey is full of small beleaguered 'islands' of natural history which have managed to survive the ravages of urban sprawl or, because of their inaccessibility, have remain unnoticed by all but a few. One of the former is Ouaisné Common, just a short walk south along the beach from of St. Brelade's bay.

It's not really a common, although the gorse, heather, willow scrub and small ponds give that impression. It's actually the remains of an ancient sand dune system which at one time stretched south-east over the ridge and down into St. Aubin's Bay. If you look carefully, you'll find the traditional flora of the sand dunes in some of the open areas kept close-cropped by rabbits.

For the naturalist, Ouaisné Common is a wonderful place to be, despite the cluster of houses climbing the steep slopes on its eastern side. It is the only place in the Channel Islands where the heather – cross-leafed heath – may be found. It supports several pairs of Dartford warblers and, unless your eye is accustomed to looking for them, you'll hear rather than see green lizards as they dive for cover. But it's the small ponds hidden deep in the gorse thickets where the interest lies in March, or at least it used to. These tiny wetland habitats, surrounded by a most unlikely mixture of vegetation, have always been the traditional stronghold of Britain's rarest amphibian – the agile frog. Sadly, the Ouaisné population has dropped to an all time low over the last decade following a succession of droughts and an insidious leaching of nitrate and nitrate-heavy water from the agricultural land above the common.

Agile frog

The good news is that in other areas of the Island, agile frogs are doing fine. The Jersey Wildlife Preservation Trust (Jersey Zoo) has laid aside an area in which to establish a breeding colony and there's a back garden not far from me in St. Clement's where, despite the noise of traffic, 'Coronation Street' and a mere concrete pond, agile frogs are breeding. They are safer at the moment in these conditions than in their natural habitat.

It was at the side of that home-made concrete pool that I discovered the most remarkable fact. At least to a nature novice like me it was remarkable and even now I'm not sure if it applies to other species. Male agile frogs, when they call during the breeding season, do so from under water.

Bob Burrow, a respected naturalist and owner of the pond, allowed me to place a finger beneath a male frog's throat during a night time filming session and, sure enough, as the sound echoed around the surrounding rockery, I distinctly felt the vibrations under my frog's chin. There was no doubt where the sound was coming from and the animal was in four inches of water.

A couple of years ago I sat in the smallest of compounds filming agile frogs. At that time they had just emerged from the water as fully fledged frogs. They were tiny yet perfect in every detail. The compound had been built by conservation ranger, Mike Freeman, as a direct result of the problems with water conditions at Ouaisné and I had been crouched in its confines like Quasimodo for about four hours when his head appeared over the fine mesh netting roof and said, "I think I'll feed them."

It seemed like a good idea until he returned fifteen minutes later with the frog food. In the bottom of a very large butterfly net was the result of swishing about in a dry hay meadow for several minutes. It was a mixture of hay seed and insects and it was one concentrated heaving mass. He opened the small trap door in the roof and proceeded to tip the contents of the net in a pile at my feet. I had never seen so many things that crawled, jumped, crept, climbed and flew, in one very confined space.

I managed to get a beautiful shot of a bright green cricket with a tail shaped like a sabre ... then the itching started. I knew it was psychosomatic but as the pile began to spread out the itching got worse and it was then I decided that I had all the pictures I needed. Some of those bugs were bigger than the frogs.

A Hint of Things to Come

Walking in the rain is sometimes quite a pleasant experience. I was on the beach at Flicquet bay, just behind St. Catherine's breakwater, and the pebble beach was a rich carpet of colours.

It's only when the stones are wet that their colours and contrasting lines and veins become apparent. On the window sill in my den I have a clear plastic box full of stones which have attracted my attention during head-down wanderings across the beach. The container is filled with water and, when the light from the lowering sun catches it, it looks like the kind of treasure chest Long John Silver would have given his other leg for.

I startled a single grey plover in breeding plumage at the Flicquet water's edge and, later, I recieved word that a wheatear has been sighted at Les Mielles on the west coast. By the time I got down there the following morning, the figure had risen to nineteen. Nice birds, wheatears, and as tough as they come. These early arrivals are on passage north from south of the Sahara desert and stop in Jersey just long enough to give us the pleasure of their upright stature and flashing white rumps before moving on.

Wheatear at St. Ouen's

I often see my first wheatear of the year on the beach at La Rocque or feeding between the fairways and the beach on Grouville Common. Every time I see them, I think of how these delicious insectivores got their name.

It would seem that the word wheatear is derived from the Saxon words 'white arse' and at times that's about all you can see of them. Just a flashing white rump disappearing over a rise. They are active, fast-moving birds of moorland and heath and are usually the first passage migrants we see. Occasionally a pair will nest in Jersey but they are not regarded as a well established breeding species here.

A Quick Flash

Driving down La Blinerie Lane this morning and the only prospect ahead: the search for a pair of shoes. Rain splattered the windsceen and it was pretty miserable. St. Helier was the last place I wanted to be.

Then, without warning, a flash of turquoise, white and orange appeared dead ahead and I was suddenly having a race down the lane with a kingfisher! I spent the rest of the shoe hunt in a sort of contented euphoria, led gently through the turmoil of town by an understanding wife.

I took a brief walk after the town expedition and March, it would appear, is becoming a bit of an old softy. There are bluebells showing amongst the daffodils, and, although not yet in great numbers, even three-cornered leek and meadow buttercups are raising an occasional head to test the weather. The palest of green young nettles, polished leaves of lords and ladies and the pungent heads of alexandre are all consenting to take the air and lawns are already lightly dusted with daisies.

Well, that's about my full repertoire of wild flowers so the rest of the year is going to be one of exploration, consulting field guides, talking to experts and filling in the enormous gaps in my knowledge of flora. I know a little but not enough. I should know more but, well I hate to say it but when I was a lad, Camberwell, south London, was not the kind of place to admit you found wild flowers interesting – unless they were featured on cigarette cards that is. Consequentely, I've got a lot of catching up to do.

A Flash of Turquoise

Hard Working Tea Spoons

I found a pair of long-tailed tits building a nest at Val de la Mare reservoir this morning and, a little later, I set up a camera and filmed their endeavours. Nick and I christened them 'teaspoons' because that's just what they look like in winter when they fly overhead.

The pair had chosen a gorse bush in which to build their lichen and cobweb nest and I set up the camera on the bracken-covered slopes beside them. I broke up the silhouette of the camcorder and tripod with a variety of available vegetation, hit the ON button, retired to the car some forty yards away, with a pair of binoculars close to hand and waited for the dust to settle.

Within a couple of minutes both birds brought building materials to the nest site and then spent several minutes commuting between the nest and a group of spritting willows whose feet were sunk in the mud of an old filter bed.

Later, when I checked the pictures, I discovered that long-tailed tits build their nests from the inside and, as the beautifully constructed homes reach the stage where they look like large grey eggs with the tops sliced off, all one can see is the bird's head literally drilling the material into the nest walls. Occasionally they both disappear deep into the bottom of the structure and push outwards. It's as if the birds are teasing the nest fabric into shape and from the outside it looks for all the world like a couple of hamsters fighting in the bottom of an old grey sock.

The end result is an absolute masterpiece of engineering.

Teaspoons

APRIL

MARCH LEFT US WITH A couple of bequests. It turned the mild westerlies into a cold northerly and added a whole hour to the light at the end of our day. I must confess that, from a naturalist's point of view, the extra light is a bonus, especially later, when evening brings moths, bats, barn owls and May bugs into the naturalist's calendar. Those summer moments are awaited with delicious anticipation.

Spring, in the meantime, is sending down its roots, opening fat buds, and blackbirds are taking it upon themselves to translate our feelings into song. From my point of view they're not doing a bad job either.

There's no doubt nature is on the move and that's what I love about April in the Island. It seems to gather momentum by the minute. The faster we advance into the month the more clues it leaves in its vibrant wake. Suddenly bumblebees are common place. There are splashes of bright red campion in the hedgerows. Hedgehog droppings on the lawn. The mallards have paired off. Many of the wintering little egret and herons have returned to mainland France and there's a robin sitting on eggs in Nick's garden.

At Pontac slip, I heard the harsh grating sound of sandwich terns on the very first day of the month. I found their raucous conversation strangely comforting. Just another indication that the natural lifecycle continues I suppose, but why do I derive such comfort from these things. It's not as if they're new. I've experienced the very same pleasure and excitement year after year without fail, and yet the feeling is forever fresh.

Red Campion

Sandwich Terns at Pontac

I've always regarded my status within this annual metamorphosis, this transition from winter into spring, as marginal. A sort of spectator standing on the side lines, and yet, I suppose simply witnessing such glorious activity must make one a part of it. Maybe it's my primitive instincts telling me that these are my roots in the same way that there's a wildlife calendar in a London office or a poster depicting 'British Whales and Dolphins' displayed in a Glasgow school. Perhaps a 'trip to the country' is making a statement. Maybe we all need to know nature's out there and that that feeling of satisfaction which seems to arise when the clocks go forward and we get out into the garden is all part of our instinctive involvement in the annual spring 'roller coaster.'

It could even be a throwback to our Neolithic forebears who probably experienced huge relief after having survived yet another hard and demanding winter. Maybe our way of translating those feelings is to get the tools out of the garden shed and join in the celebrations.

Pondering

April in Jersey is a superb month for migrant birds passing through the Island and among the earliest are the sand martins. I counted a dozen or so performing aerobatics and hunting for newly hatched fly along the thick margin of phragmites reed surrounding St. Ouen's Pond today.

The explosive sound of a cetti's warbler gave the tall reeds life and a male lapwing was performing the most amazing in-flight gyrations just, I suspect, to impress his intended. There's a small hide built into the bank overlooking the pond. It can't be seen from the road but if you follow the narrow path through the tussocks and over the brow you won't miss it. Inside there's a book and pen provided by the Société Jersiaise so that sightings may be recorded. That kind of record is fine, I suppose, for those who keep lists, make counts, draw graphs and eventually arrive at a clearer picture of Island bird movements. But for the general observer it is a constant source of enormous frustration. For example, during those early April days when, for one reason or another, I couldn't get to the pond, I missed a blue throat, eleven avocets, a marsh harrier, at least two male bearded reedlings performing like mad. And, according to the book, a quick sortie into France allowed me to neatly avoid the only osprey sighted in the Island for some considerable time. I appreciate that the more hours you spend in the great outdoors the more you see but when it comes to birding, the episodes I miss always seem to be the most important.

I'm not sure that having the opportunity to read about what you've missed is a good thing. The temptation, of course, is to make a clear and precise entry stating, 'Single spoon-billed sandpiper feeding on scrape. Small flock of imperial eagles overflew pond. Two smews, three masked lapwings and a greater flamingo feeding at pond. Male fan-tailed warbler perched on edge of hide. Weather: Fine. Visibility: Perfect. PS: Bet you wished you'd been here!' and leave a totally illegible signature. But of course, we don't do it. Do we?

Avocets, St. Ouen's Bay

Wild Island

For three successive days the Island has been shrouded in thick fog and yet, during that time, literally thousands of swallows and house martins have arrived. They really are an amazing sight. One minute there are none and the next the air is swarming with feeding birds. I can only assume they dip down through the fog to feed and then continue their journey above it. These birds were passing through of course. Jersey's residents will arrive a little later in the month. Those passage migrants will probably carry on up through the UK, turning off at their favourite farm in the Yorkshire Dales, flit comfortably over a midge-filled lochan somewhere in the north-west of Scotland or just spend a pleasant summer season in Plymouth. It's good to let the imagination run riot sometimes, preferably in a traffic jam or when the day-job becomes less than grippingly interesting.

House Guests

What I wanted to know was how did the house spider find out about my new garden shed. There were spiders in the old shed, big black hairy jobbies which fell out of everything I touched. Pick up an old winter sock or a box of unemployed Star Wars figures and out they came, scuttling off under the everlasting Christmas tree. Yes, it was one of those sheds. It took a day and two bottles of Muscadet to put up and about two hours to fill with spider habitat. Are garden spiders actually house spiders waiting for the chance to 'squat' or do house spiders look out of the window and think 'Ah! A new garden shed – just right for Blodwyn and Kevin'. Then out they come, over the grass and through the flower beds like some old-fashioned safari, in through the cracks in the tongue-and-groove and there they are, all ready for a 'junk warming' party.

My book, *The Natural History of Britain and Europe*, tells me that the house spider – and there are several species – loves out-houses and such. That's fine, but before I put up the first shed there *were* no out-houses. I think I'll stick with my original theory of house spiders keeping an eye – or is it eyes – open for the main chance.

Hard to Swallow

There was a swallow sighted on the first day of this vibrant month, all fork tailed and fancy free, strutting his stuff at La Rocque harbour on the east coast. That's a bit early even for these dinner-jacketed hirundines.

While we're on the subject of swallows I wonder who penned that old chestnut about 'a single swallow not making a summer.' Talk about stating the obvious. In my humble opinion 'a single swallow' is lost, and about as useful a seasonal indicator as the sundial is at divulging the correct time. Swallows, according to my records, arrive in mid-April and that's spring, not summer.

If you want a bird that says ' Here comes summer' look for the swift. Swifts eat insects and most of these insects simply don't fly until it's warm. Swifts eat insects who consider it warm. On several occasions I've recorded individual swallows mooching about my meadow in early December with that 'I wonder where all the lads have gone' look about them. What do swallows know?

Easter Spring Tides

Last night there was a full moon. This morning the sea reached the very top of every beach and slipway. It's a spring tide and from low water the sea has risen a full thirty-eight feet. The heaps of old seaweeds, stranded by the last big tides and blackened by weeks of wind and sun are being tossed by the inshore swell and the sandfly grubs washed from the drowned piles are providing a prodigious feast for Brent geese, herring gulls; even a pair of mallard tucked in to the feast with great relish.

So far up the beach did the moon's gravity pull the early morning surge that the flies which had already hatched were driven off the beach and onto the sea wall. At one point, at La Rocque harbour, the wall was literally black with them. Starlings frantically fed on them and even a robin commuted back and forth with fly-filled bill to feed a mate in a seaside garden nest. A single pied wagtail sat in the middle of a cloud of flies totally replete, so dense was the airborne larder.

There are still winter migrants on the off-shore rocks along the east coast, many beginning to change into breeding plumage. The sanderlings are looking decidedly off-white compared to their smart white winter dress and many of the dunlin have that lovely black patch under their bellies. Common terns were there too, looking as elegant and delightful as ever. Nice to think that in order to give me the pleasure of their company at Pontac slip, on the south-east corner of Jersey, they could well have flown the full length of the African and European continents.

Down Among the Reefs

When this spring tide recedes in the afternoon, low water fishermen will be looking for a crop of ormers. Ormers are molluscs with a single shell lined on the inside with deliciously delicate mother of pearl. They are regarded as a delicacy in Jersey and, for those who know how to cook them, that's exactly what they are. But the best way to enjoy ormers is to take on the tough job of finding them and then, *if* you work hard enough to harvest a half-dozen or so, you'll have earned the pleasure of their unique flavour.

When I was younger, a veritable fleet of small craft headed for the Minquiers reef on Spring tides to gather ormers. The boats, usually a fleet substantial enough to satisfy a Dunkirk veteran, would off-load their passengers onto a rocky moon-scape laid bare only on the lowest of spring tides, and, armed with ormer hooks, wicker baskets and a primordial hunting instinct, each fisherman would melt into the dank kelpy canyons to turn boulders, search the darkest of crevices and reach beneath submerged cave-like holes. Such places could provide a rich feast but only for those prepared to wade chest-deep in water which had not yet felt the benefit of summer sun.

The Ormer

These ormering tides were hard work made even harder by the fact that fishing time amongst the lagoons and boulder-strew network of reefs stretching sixteen miles through the bay of St. Malo was limited to two or three hours. Catches, depending on equal quantities of skill and luck, could range from several dozen ormers to a complete blank. On the return trip the 'chill factor' was fought with Thermos flasks filled with heavily laced coffee and sometimes with just the 'lace'. I can't remember anyone suggesting jumping up and down to keep warm!

In the 1960s a dozen ormers would fetch about a pound sterling. Today the same feed of ormers would set you back the price of a four course restaurant dinner ... unless you're prepared to roll up your sleeves and do a little DIY fishing.

Wild Wood Walking

Already almost two-thirds of this glorious month have gone. It's a frantic, yet blissful time of year. The temptation, especially when it comes to 'birding', is to cover as much ground as possible during the month in case you miss something. The 'observations book' at the St. Ouen's Pond hide is proof enough that you can only be in one place at a time and miss birds you undoubtedly will.

Nick and I took a *gentle* voyage into April today. No rush, just a quiet walk into Rosel woods with the appropriate field guide and all the time in the world. Most of the common deciduous trees can be found here and the occasional rarity such as the medlar, a rather unassuming, fruit-bearing tree, pretty much on the edge of its northern range. I've yet to find one but Nick, and the illustrated and weather-proofed notices placed strategically along this most popular of walks, assure me that they are there.

The wood is set in a deep clefted valley which climbs gently towards the west. On its floor a brook winds down rills and secret little glides, emptying into a small reservoir. There are trout, freshwater shrimp and eels in the brook and the reservoir is the haunt of big carp, tench and rudd but our attention on this occasion was drawn to the damp and shady woodland with its steep climbing banks where kestrel, jay and red squirrel enjoy dappled clearings and willow-shaded marshy places.

The oaks have barely unfurled their brand new ochre and burnt orange leaves but the wild cherries and blackthorns are in blossom and, much to our delight, there was a variety of wild flowers beginning to show.

As we moved through the still morning we discussed nature's taste in spring colour, comparing it with that of our own parks, gardens and meticulously laid out sea-front flower beds. Civic pride seems bent on a furious display of colour, no doubt a celebration of the end of a drab, wet winter. Nature, we decided, was a little more subtle in her choice of colours and, frankly, we much prefer them.

At one point in the wood there was a bank of bluebells, wood sorrel and celandine – blue, white and yellow couched in a delicate mixture of fresh April greens. Yellow is a colour fairly representative of spring in these quiet woods. We saw archangel, the palest of late wild daffodils and, in the dampest areas, saxifrage undulated over the ground like an enormous gold and green duvet.

Occasionally, the pale blue of dog violets caught the eye and in the shady verges herb

Wood Sorrel

robert and stitchwort added to an ever growing list.

The way sycamore logs had been stacked, after being cut down to allow patches of sunlight to penetrate the woodland floor, was interesting. Retaining stakes had been driven into the ground at the edge of the path on either side of piles of thick branch poles and, over two or three years, these had gradually subsided. Now mosses, fungi and ferns have taken up residence. I suspect that the base of the pile provides food and shelter for mammals and insects too. In the long term this stacking method seems almost as beneficial to nature as leaving a tree where it falls and allowing it to degenerate naturally.

It's strange how dead wood is such a wonderful host to wildlife. Last year I moved a large pile of beech logs from a nearby store up to my home and, within a week or so, the most amazing groups of polished, china-like fungus appeared. It was, my field guide told me, porcelain fungus. It was edible and it was rare. I didn't doubt the book but neither did I cook the fungus.

Meanwhile, back in the woods, the path took us high up above the edge of the valley and into the upper canopy of the trees. We found ourselves on equal terms with chiffchaffs, ear to ear with a very vociferous blackcap and on the flight path of a single-minded mistle thrush. Up here, where the sun gained easier access to the woodland floor, red campion began to appear along the banks and, at the very top of the path, in a grassy suntrap, the white heads of bladder campion flowered in profusuion against a background of gloriously golden gorse. That was indeed a voyage into April !

On the High Ground

Later in the year the heathland of Les Landes will produce the most wonderful carpet of heather. At the moment, however, it's the gorse that stands four-square, centre-stage. It *is* spectacular and, given a calm day, the smell of coconut is positively intoxicating. The pink blush of cock linnet breasts is claiming more and more spiky song posts and meadow pipits are lifting like skylarks over this north-westerly landcape. It's a place for walking. A place where the everyday sounds are absent and the sky seems to go on for ever. Later in the year we'll revisit Les Landes. It has an atmosphere that would have made Thomas Hardy feel at home.

MAY

I HAD SAT STARING AT the word' May', written in bold capitals at the top of the computer screen, for about twenty minutes. Then I decided that the only way to write an introduction to my favourite month was to get out amongst it despite the rain and fog.

It was a curlew that finally persuaded me. It came slanting in through the misty rain from the sea past my den window and, on hollowed wings, landed in the egret meadow. It then produced that most nostalgic of sounds and I simply couldn't resist it.

A few minutes later, booted and wax jacketed, with a pair of binoculars bouncing on my chest, I was climbing out of a rather moribund state of mind and into May, largely thanks to a curlew that shouldn't really have been there in the first place.

The first thing to greet me was that delicious sound that I'd not heard since last Autumn – rain on leaves. There's no sound quite like it, especially at that moment when it first catches the attention. It was accompanied by uninhibited bird song ranging from talkative blackbirds to wrens full of their own importance and a chiffchaff that only seemed to get his song right some of the time.

Curlew

By Any Other Name

The woods above the house were carpeted with bluebells and patches of three-cornered leeks and, for the umpteenth time in as many seasons I thought what a totally absurd name this is for a flower... "Here you are darling, I've brought you a bunch of three-cornered leeks." I'll grant that on close examination the stems of these white, bell-shaped flowers (you could be forgiven for thinking they were white bluebells) are triangular, which is where the name comes from. And they *are* members of the leek family – the smell of spring onions when the flowers are picked confirms this – but, visually, I think they deserve better.

There are other names that fall slightly short of picturesque in nature too, don't you find. Lump-sucker is a ghastly example. A veritable injustice in the world of descriptive

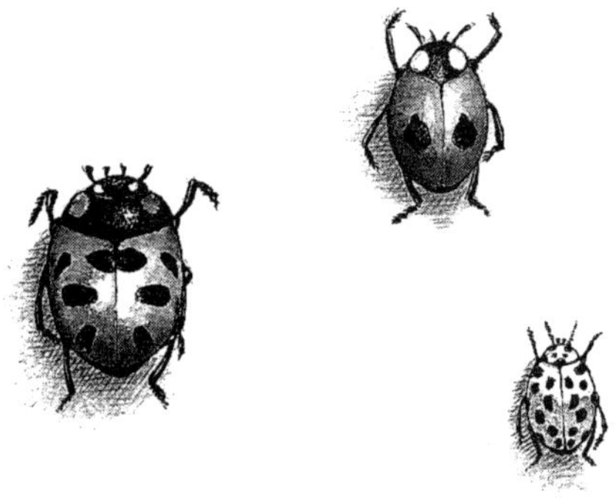

marine classification. This rotund, rather knobbly fish is a splendid character. There is an alternative colloquial name – the 'sea hen', which is a much kinder and gentler name but no, officially, it's a lump-sucker.

Imagine some poor angler at a dinner party producing the gem, 'I hold the British lump-sucker record you know.' Hostess departs with a fit of the giggles, rest of party make poor attempts at keeping straight faces.

I once had the same kind of reaction on announcing I had seen two bearded tits at Radipole Reserve in Weymouth. I'm sure they thought I was some kind of voyeur – the dinner party that is, not the birds. Possibly in order to avoid embarrassment to birdwatchers and fits of mass choking at dinner parties, the species has now been re-named the bearded reedling. A purely scientific adjustment I understand.

A 'twenty-four spotted ladybird' seems a masterly piece of non-creative classification too. I'm not a 'net-swishing entomologist', so counting spots on the backs of ladybirds that happen to be sitting on a nettle is always a problem. Most of my observations concerning the seriously spot-endowed species involve either the eighteen- or nineteen-spotted varieties and before you grab the reference book, I should warn you that they don't exist. That's just the number I usually manage to count before they fly off, which in turn means I never get to know whether my specimen was a twenty-two spotted or a twenty-four-spotted bug. Well even a ladybird's patience can be stretched.

During a brief lull in my mental consideration of natural appellations such as dog violets, ivy-leafed toadflax and 'left-handed jewel boxes' (the latter is a sort of spiny cockle), I decided to spend an hour or two on the west coast, at Les Mielles. It provided just the tonic I needed because, although April had been an interesting month in terms of wildlife, the weather had been extremely dull.

I'm one of those animals that notices the absence of sunlight, partly, I suppose, because of my camera work, but I get a mental craving for it after a sustained period of overcast conditions whether I want to film or not. So much so that a flight to Heathrow and a twenty minute burst of sun up above the clouds has restored my mood on more than one occasion. Just knowing it's there is enough.

On this morning in early May, I actually drove out of the overcast and into the sun and by the time I had parked, close by St. Ouen's Pond, the day was bright, my inner thoughts were giving way to the activity around me and, to compound a growing contentment, there

Three-cornered Leek

were two swifts flickering among the hirundines over the pond. My cup positively overflowed.

Birds make excellent seasonal milestones and, as I lay on the bank overlooking the water, a cetti's warbler began the opening bars of 'William Tell' (the Lone Ranger bit) and several reed warblers were chuckling away in the sedge too. Over towards Mielles de Morville a magpie gave a magnificent aerial display while in hot pursuit of a cuckoo and the remains of my moribund state finally evaporated with the demise of April weather.

Swifts over St. Ouen's Pond

Booby Trapped

A week into May and the change in the weather had consolidated. The temperatures soared, there was little or no wind to cool the air and grass cutting was becoming a serious consideration. Fortunately, the phone rang and the voice at the other end said that if I were to present myself at Bouley Bay at eleven-thirty that morning with camera and equipment, a chance to film gannets was in the offing. The state of the grass faded into oblivion.

The sea was almost unruffled and I could see huge patches of totally smooth water over the shoulder of the rubber-suited helmsman. The boat, a very large semi-inflatable, was rollicking along at around 45mph which meant that Alderney and the adjacent gannet colony at Garden Rocks were a mere three-quarters of an hour ahead.

Several guillimots, a solitary Manx shearwater and the bow wave of a Brittany Ferries' car carrier later, I was dumped without too much ceremony and even less dignity at the base of a lump of steeply sloping granite some forty yards from the main bird colony at Garden Rocks.

Surrounded by gear on the dank and narrow confines of a low tide ledge, I listened to the sound of my lift fading into the distance and hoped the weather and the swell wouldn't change over the next four hours.

The sky was filled with birds and yet any sounds from the main colony were muffled by the massive rock I was climbing. As I neared the ridge, overlooking the gannetry, the sound intensified and so did the smell. I lifted my head very gently over the crest so as not to disturb the birds. Fat chance! There was no great panic, no nervous birds taking off in fear and trepidation. Frankly, and delightfully, I was ignored.

From then on my stay with this huge bird community was like one of those armchair wildlife documentaries. Through the camera lens I watched the gannets' greeting display, the gentle clashing of dagger-like bills. I recorded the precision with which the nests were designed and spaced and the skill with which these great oceanic birds managed to land in confined spaces despite a six-foot wing span. The general overcrowding would have made a City Council blush.

For so gentle a bird, the gannet has the most wicked looking blue eyes and the dark lines running back from the tip of the bill give them a decidedly fierce appearence. Another peculiarity is that they have no external nostrils. I actually failed to notice this when I was filming but read it later, in less demanding circumstances. This lack of nostril holes is an adaptation enabling them to dive into the water from heights of up to a hundred feet when hunting. Having suffered from sinus trouble myself, I can see nature's reason for customising the bill. Salt water up the nose at 80 mph *would* be inclined to make the eyes water a bit!

The gannet's nest building material was, sadly, a reflection on our own careless disregard for the sea. Part of the construction *was* seaweed, the traditional source of building material. Birds were bringing it to the nest sites constantly but the weed was hardly noticeable compared to bits of nylon rope, in every conceivable colour, plastic strapping from bales and cardboard boxes, the plastic circles from beer can packs, monofiliment fish netting, plastic carrier bags and lumps of polystyrene.

Several birds wore orange necklaces made from strands of polypropelene rope. They seemed to manage well enough but what shocked me most was the number of birds with black oil smears on their breasts. These were birds which would be termed 'lightly oiled' and I supposed they should be regarded as lucky. But it led me to consider just what damage must be occurring out there on the oceans' surface, beyond sight of land.

There were several shag nests on my rock, all complete with eggs and sitting birds. They were quite delightful with their 'punk' like crests and deep, deep bottle-green plumage outlined with a scaly pattern reminiscent of their lizard ancestors. There were several guillimot nests too and the birds were fearless on my approach. I always think they are about the closest I'll ever get to seeing penguins first-hand.

I spent the return thirty-two mile journey keeping a weather eye open for bottle-nosed dolphins but, as wide as the calm sea was, there was no sign of their sleek black backs. A brilliant day, nevertheless, and one I shall always cherish.

Overleaf: Gannets at Garden Rocks

Wren Den

At last I've found that elusive wren's nest in my 'wild' garden. A year ago the family embarrassed me by building in the most unexpected place. I'd set up a permanent hide in the garden overlooking a small pond. The plan was to film from the hide and in a moment of inspiration, I had surrounded it with chicken wire and filled it with bracken, privet cuttings and anything else that would help soften the sharp edges. From its unintrusive confines I spent a great number of hours trying to discover the whereabouts of my resident wren's cave. In late autumn I found it, built into the side of the hide.

This year the wrens have set up home in a typical wren location and, naturally, it's the last place I would have looked in the normal course of events. Only the disposal of a barrow-load of strimmed grass cuttings under the hedge revealed the nest and it was so *obviously* the right place. A perfect, slightly elongated affair, clinging to three branches of a hawthorn, a couple of feet off the ground.

Meadow Sweet

The egret meadow is flushed with colour. A casual glance shows ragged robin and cuckoo flowers with yellow flag iris under the scrub oak where it's really marshy. A closer look revealed a deliciously purple tinge showing through the grasses – loose flowering or Jersey orchid is begining to show.

It's necessary either to follow the path into the field or use binoculars in order to appreciate them. They are a delicate early bloom and, because the stems are as purple as the flower spray, the colour seems to be strengthened, especially towards the end of the month when they are most numerous and at their best. In fact the flower heads are so dark that they make the ragged robin accompanying them pale into insignificance.

There are still egrets among the oaks and willow but their numbers have decreased considerably compared to the winter months and only a couple of herons are sharing the roost.

Coastal Encounters

The thrift is crowding the roadsides along the Five Mile Road at the moment and there are scarlet pimpernel and masses of buttercups and daisies carpeting the meadows on the landward side.

Wild Island

Tree mallow is in bloom too and while waiting for a wall brown butterfly to settle for the camera, I couldn't help noticing what an attraction the mallow is for insects. Bumblebees were regular visitors *and* honey bees. Damselflies were hovering over the crown and a myriad of ants and other insects filled the insides of some of the blooms.

Hottentot fig is in bloom and the flowers, a mixture of delicate yellows, creams and pinks are crowding the sunny, sloping sides of old German bunkers. This recently introduced plant is proving to be a mixed blessing. The flowers and foliage are unarguably beautiful and, to the casual observer, look perfectly natural and attractive. Unfortunately the plant, with its heavy, succulent leaves, is covering much of the south coast cliffs and over the last two decades has begun to destroy the habitat of other coastal plants.

No other plant life seems capable of sharing the ground overrun by hottentot fig except, perhaps, previously established gorse and broom. It makes great demands on the limited moisture available on the steeper cliffs and birds enjoy no benefit from its foliage as far as I can make out. In fact, if anything, it seems to be slowly pushing gulls and oyster-catchers off their traditional nesting sites and is becoming a serious threat to the established habitat.

Jersey Orchid

Tadpoles Apart

I went to a meeting last night that gave me an up-date on my earlier agile frog notes. It was disturbing because it revealed that, following a spring search for the species, conservationists are now convinced that few, if any, are breeding in the wild anywhere in the Island.

The good news, however, is that the captive breeding stock is alive and well. It is also reaching a stage where, at some point soon, it will have to be released or provided with larger accommodation. As this month of May draws to a close frantic efforts are being made to provide sites and pens for thousands of tadpoles that are rapidly developing into juvenile frogs. The pens have been designed to keep predators out and allow insect life in (as a food source) while the young frogs reach a stage where they can be released with a good chance of survival. They should also provide the time needed to find clean water sites where new breeding colonies can be established.

I learned a great deal about agile frogs at that meeting. Take predators for example. In their water environment, fish, newts and dragonfly larvae will prey on tadpoles and, when they emerge as fully-fleged frogs, their problems are only just beginning. Most garden birds will eat them, including blackbirds, song-thrushes and robins because when they first leave the water they are about as big as the average thumb nail. The predator list is endless – herons, egrets, all the crow family, rats, cats, stoats, polecats and ferrets to name but a few. When their natural breeding habitat, water, becomes an untrustworthy element, the odds are really stacked against them.

These pens should buy time for the species. Some local naturalists are convinced that unless the current stock can be reared and reintroduced into a natural habitat, especially after two disastrous breeding season in the wild preceeded by several years of drought, the agile frog could be lost as a breeding species in Britain. The story will continue.

Coastal Colour

Work took me to the sand dunes at Les Mielles this morning, in search of the dwarf pansy – actually more microscopic than dwarf. I didn't find the flower I wanted but I couldn't think of a better place to be in late May with the sun warming my shoulders and visibility as clear as crystal.

The dunes were an absolute picture. The ground was carpeted with cream-coloured burnet rose. Wide patches of speedwell stained the sides of the sandy paths while horse-shoe vetch and evening primrose added a splash of yellow to the steep sloping banks. There was freshly unfurled bracken and spurge and lichens and tiny dove's-foot cranesbill caught my eye. Overhead the uninhibited song of a very happy skylark fell to earth like the glitter of a spent firework.

Giving up the fruitless search for the fabled pansy, I actually drove past my favourite hostelry, the La Pulente pub, leaving a perfectly good pint of Bass in my wake, and headed for Gorselands on the south coast – such dedication.

The transition from dunes to cliffs is amazing and in Jersey it can be accomplished, literally, within minutes. The flora and the birds are totally different and the sounds are as from another world.

Gorselands has been acquired as a nature reserve and is managed by the Island's Environment and Country Services Department. There is now a pathway stretching from La Corbière to Beauport which follows the cliff path *through* Gorselands. The cliffs and off-shore stacks are more gentle on this southerly coast and the colour of the granite is a soft pink. It's a good place for nesting ravens in early spring and at least one pair of barn owls has taken advantage of a natural fissure in the rock face and they breed there regularly.

The flora in early summer on Gorselands' rocky slopes inspired Nick to base a delicious set of commissioned Jersey postage stamps on the flowers found there. The area is a natural rockery supporting sheepsbit scabious, spotted rock rose, white campion and thrift as well as ox-eye daisy, common gorse, prostrate broom and the brightly coloured lichens. It's hard to believe now but the area came within an ace of becoming a golf course.

Nick found the dwarf pansies. It's amazing what a little incentive will do for the powers of observation. All I said was, "If you find any that are filmable I'll buy you a pint." Minutes later he was back with a grin on his face asking what time the pubs opened.

They really *are* small, dwarf pansies. Fortunately there were burnet roses in the background which put their size into some kind of perspective. Size comparison when you're shooting wildlife subjects is always a bit of a problem unless there's a convenient insect or two in the neighbourhood – much better than a ballpoint pen tip, or a fifty pence piece or a rabbit dropping.

Cuckoo

JUNE

When I surveyed the shoreline at La Rocque there was an uncanny silence. No piping of grey plover and no sign of turnstones climbing mounds of vraic. The winter waders had gone and there was a silence on the east coast which, in an odd sort of way, announced summer. Apart from a few gulls mooching about and a solitary common tern, the place was deserted.

I should have realised, because a few days earlier, as I sipped a last drink beside the dying embers of the first barbecue of the year, half a dozen Brent geese flew over the house heading east. As a rule I never see them from home and I guessed they were taking a short cut over St. Clement to Siberia. Well that's what I thought at the time, helped, I suspect, by the mellowing effects of good company and a large malt whisky. They were the last birds I saw and I don't expect them back until mid-September. When they return, I'll no doubt drink their health again.

Departing Brents

Wild Island

I always have a wistful sense of loss when the shore birds have gone but it never lasts for long on two counts. Firstly there's the comfort of knowing that, within a few months early birds, the scouts for the main flocks, will begin returning and, secondly, during that hiatus period the sea itself will be filled with summer migrants and I've been a fisherman since I was six.

'Wall' Flowers

At the moment Jersey is a picture. The tops of granite walls are bursting with valerian in pink, red and, occasionally, white. They are such a prolific flowering plant in Jersey and they grow in the most unlikely places. I once saw one in full bloom behind a street name in St. Helier. The street was called 'Garden Lane.'

"The trouble with valerian," observed Nick, "is that it only grows by accident. It doesn't seem to like the comfort of a flower bed."

If Island walls are anything to go by, he's right, of course, and that's what makes it so attractive. I know it's not loved by the owners of nice granite structures that probably require repointing but, well, long may it bloom. It's very much a part of early summer.

There are masses of meadow buttercups in the hedgerows at the moment, with hawthorn and elderflower blooms dusting the crowns higher up and, today, I saw several farm workers cutting back the grasses that hurl themselves out of the ground at this time of year and turn already narrow lanes into mere footpaths. What impressed me so much was that they were using sickles! Frankly I was delighted. I detest those tractor flails which systematically destroy healthy trees and ruin perfectly good hedgerows. Maybe they're effective in skilled hands but in most cases they cause havoc.

On the Hover

Hover-flies don't sting

In my wild garden hover-flies are either hanging in the dappled shade or parked on fresh green bramble leaves and it's good to see them. It's even better since I discovered they really are flies, not wasps, despite their black and yellow colouring and, what's more, they don't sting !

Since I discovered that nugget of information I've taken a closer interest in them. I've always admired their flying skills and recently I've been offering them an up-turned hand. Occasionally they'll inspect each finger individually and even land for a moment giving me a chance to take a closer look. I'm sure there must be half-a-dozen species in the garden judging by the variation in their shape, size and colours.

So far, I've recorded speckled wood, peacock, holly blue, common blue and painted lady butterflies enjoying the fruits of my very meagre gardening efforts. Apart from an access path, my wild garden sort of looks after itself *and* plants itself too. This year it's blessed with balm-leafed figwort which I certainly didn't plant and a cluster of tall spiky teasel which the greenfinches will love. The pond, which originally only supported sedge, wild yellow iris and water-lilies, now boasts purple loosestrife, water-cress, duckweed and what looks like great spearwort.

I have a couple of log stools by the pond. It's a place to ponder, if you'll excuse the pun, and ever since the day I filled it with good old tap water it's been a source of enormous pleasure – toads in early spring, water beetles, water boatmen, newts, dragonfly larvae, three kinds of damselfly, leeches and more species of flies than a dog has fleas. I just can't imagine a garden without a pond.

Lepidoptery Revisited

This year's first painted lady was no doubt a migrant and was probably helped on her, or his, way (they both look alike) into my garden by a warm southerly wind. They apparently hibernate in southern Europe and North Africa and when they set out for northern climes the species can reach Iceland in a good year. I have to admit that the painted lady I saw was rather faded and I'm not surprised considering the distance she'd travelled. Where does such a small animal find so much energy?

One other point which made me feel a bit better about the state of my 'wild garden' was the fact that these big, bold, international travellers enjoy thistles and stinging nettles. Good! My bit of garden should attract quite a few this year.

Looking back to when I was a lad, there was an art in catching butterflies. You'd take your blazer off and wade through the hay meadow with it spread out in front of you with the collar tucked under you chin and, when you saw a butterfly, and if you were close enough, you would dive full length, smothering the unfortunate creature under the blazer. When the coat was carefully peeled back, there it would be, pinned down by the flattened grasses. It would then be carefully transferred to a good sturdy jam jar for further scrutiny and the lid would have holes in so the captured insect could breathe. You'd even put some grass and flower in too, in case it got hungry.

I often reflect on those early hunting expeditions into hay meadows and the time spent delving into the grey mud of seaside harbours for specimens. I was certainly driven by curiosity and the need to get closer to nature. I certainly got closer to butterflies than most in those days. Thankfully very little has changed apart from knowing I can get muddy now without getting a thick ear although, regrettably, I've lost that delicate touch which enabled me to pick up a butterfly without damaging it.

A good, sturdy jam-jar

I never really gave the butterfly much thought after those trouble-free days of evacuation to the country – Spitfires, Lockheed Lightnings and Bren gun carriers got in the way. *Now*, of course, I find them delightful and I'm rediscovering the fascination of those early days all over again. These days I only watch them. Dignity and old bones have seen to that and rediscovering them has been a joy.

At this time of year the number of species flying is quite low but, nevertheless, there will be a few that may well find you thumbing through your field guide. Sheltered corners among the headlands at La Corbière, L'Oeillière and the bramble-filled depressions of Les Landes are excellent places to find the green hairstreak, a small butterfly about the size of the common blue. The male is painted in a shade of green that needs to be seen to be believed. I've not found a single plant foliage that comes close to matching the colour of this delicate little insect, yet despite a vibrant green verging on fluorescent, the hairstreak may remain totally undetected until it's either disturbed or shows its pugnacity to other butterflies.

At the northern end of Les Mielles high up on the escarpment there's a five-thousand year-old passage grave called Dolmen Des Monts, Grantez. It lies in about twenty-seven acres of National Trust land and is used for rough grazing at certain times of the year. It's a mixture of grasses, bracken, nettle and ragwort and in late June it's the perfect place to see the cinnabar moth, a bold black and red day-time moth with the reputation for being the most poisonous in Britain. Look for the cinnabar caterpillars too. They are hooped with orange and black stripes and feed happily on ragwort and groundsel. Both these food plants are rich in alkaloid poisons which are transferred to chrysalis and moth during metamorphosis, making them extremely poisonous to reptiles, mammals and birds. Well there we are! Cinnabar moths are nice to see but for goodness sake repress the temptation to eat one!

Lounge Lizard

At last there's some serious heat in the sun. The breeze has lost that uncomfortable edge and 'short sleeve order' is safe. I'm not the only one enjoying the sun either. I've caught more than one green lizard unawares recently on the west coast, basking on the soft sand of the dunes. It's an odd thing about green lizards, once you know what they look like – size, colour, texture and such – they're easy enough to see, but until some kind soul points one out to you, these beautiful creatures just blend in and are totally invisible.

There was a time when I desperately needed some shots of these big, emerald-green reptiles, and for several weeks I'd carted a broadcast camcorder, several batteries and a heavy duty tripod up hill and down dale in hot pursuit of *lacerta viridis*, all to no avail.

Plenty of rustling in the marram grass and disappearing tails. Plenty of advice from people who'd 'seen thousands' but I still had a blank tape, a slimmer profile and a distinct feeling that me and these elusive green dragons were destined never to meet.

Success finally came in the lounge of the La Pulente pub. Nigel, the landlord, had just bought a video camera and the moment he saw me dump mine on his lounge carpet there was an immediate air of camaraderie. All I wanted was a quiet pint and a serious think. I needed lizards 'in the can' but couldn't find any. I suppose I must have looked a bit disgruntled.

"What's the problem?" asked Nigel, sliding the second pint and a steak sandwich across the bar.

" I can't find any b...... lizards ! That's the problem!

I explained the extent of my fruitless searchings and, in exchange for explaining the difference between his camera and mine (about £30,000), Nigel put me right.

He looked at his watch, had a quick word with the barmaid and pronounced the unforgettable legend, "Give me five minutes and I'll show you some."

And he did. And I filmed them, close-up. And they did everything but wear make-up!

They were on a cliff-side path edged with old railway sleepers, blackberry bushes, wild honeysuckle and bracken. The path was cut deep by summer-sandled feet and the lizards were amazingly tolerant. They were simply accustomed to people constantly using the narrow footpath that led to some magnificent views over St. Ouen's Bay.

A pint of Bass and a landlord with a penchant for home movies provided me with all the green lizard pictures I needed. I came to the conclusion that I should have drunk more and haunted the sand dunes of Les Blanches Banques less. It would have saved hundreds of hours of fruitless endeavour and might even have improved my crib game.

An elusive lizard

Of Birds and Nests

That nice convenient period during April and May, when birds were active and could be *seen* to be active, because the foliage on the trees was negligible, has gone the way of all springs. Now, dense undergrowth, impenetrable trees and thickening hedgerows was all making activity within hard to observe. From the nesting bird's point of view, that's how it should be. From my point of view it has become very difficult to be nosy. I'm a bit past wriggling through thickets these days and the pollen count plays havoc with the old nasal passages but I have to confess I've never lost the habits of my youth. My nesting abilities might not as razor-sharp, but I still get the urge to search a likely robin or dunnock's lair, discreetly, of course.

Such was the case recently when Nick and I did a little gentle prying. In most cases the nests had served their purpose. Take the mistle-thrushes' nest for example.

It was in the fork of a large and very healthy lime tree and no more than five feet off the ground. A great bulky affair designed to contain a crowd of demanding fledglings for several weeks. It was in perfect condition and so firmly set in the fork that it might have been glued there.

I shall wait until later in the season and find out exactly how it clings to the tree so well. I suspect the foundations are somehow woven into the bark.

There's a wren nesting in a hole in the wall of the colombière at Samarès manor. I can only assume the hole is much bigger than the entrance because the nest material is hardly visible. Nick has a wren building a nest in one of his tit boxes too. All very strange. Stranger still is the recent report of a goldfinch building in a great tit nest box. What is the world coming to?

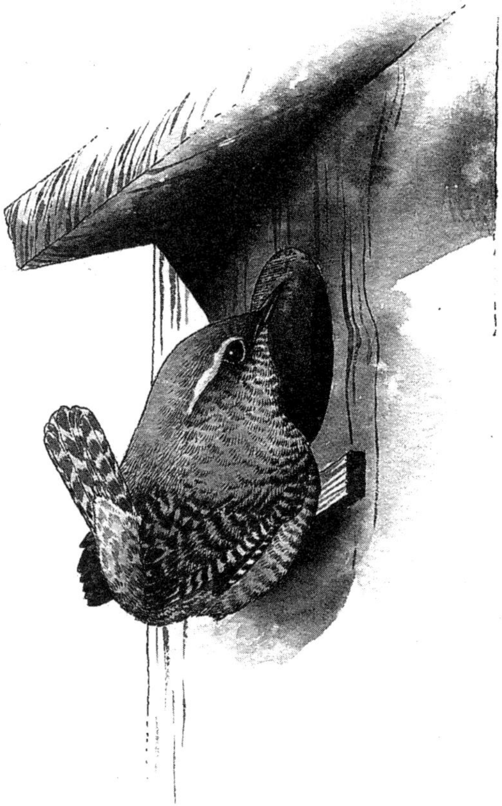

House-hunting Wren

Stumped

I'd just been filming great spotted woodpeckers in St. Catherine's Wood and, on the way back to the car, came face to face with Nick. He'd found a photographable kestrel's nest on a rocky ledge further up the valley and was on his way to the site. As we quietly chatted by the old German reservoir I glanced over Nick's shoulder and saw the tree stump, protruding from the water about ten feet from the bank, move.

At first I thought it was *cameraman's eye* – you know, too much peering through the lens – but the stump moved again and I pointed out the phenomenon to Nick. Sitting on the moss-covered top of the stump, legs akimbo, neck out-stretched enjoying the early morning sun, was a large terrapin, totally oblivious both to our presence and our amazement.

As we watched the animal basking in the ever growing heat I searched my mind for any relevant information on terrapins. Net result, zero.

Subsequent inquiries told me that it was a Mississippi red-eared terrapin, sometimes known as a red-eared slider and probably introduced into the Island's water system by some disillusioned pet owner. There could be a number living contentedly in the wild, as the result of mild winters and the importation of several species by aquarists and pet shops. I got quite excited about the sighting but my enthusiasm was quenched on discovering that as far as terrapin spotting enthusiasts are concerned, they are a fairly familiar sight. I'm sure I walk about with my eyes closed sometimes although on this occasion I shot some interesting footage.

Has Beans

My meadow is filled with bean poles and so much plastic mesh it looks like mist. The crop will be runner beans and the plants are already climbing the plastic netting. By the end of the month the whole field will be green, hazed with tiny red blooms. This is the second year the crop has been planted. Last year, at the end of the season, I wondered how they would manage to untangle all the old plants and save the plastic for another year. How naive can you get. They must have sprayed the crop with something highly virulent because within two weeks there wasn't the smallest patch of green left, just brown, crispy deadness. The plastic was burned.

Spider Rider

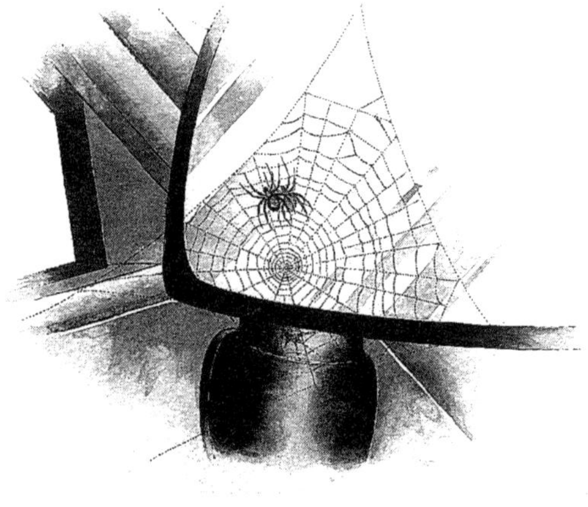

Neugene

I thought I asked enough questions *before* setting about writing this journal but, since I began, I've looked closer, noticed more and the result has been a considerable increase on the questions front, the answers to many of which are not in the reference books.

How, for instance, did the *first* bluetit discover that there was cream under the tin foil cap of a milk bottle and how did that bird manage to pass on the good news? How did the *first* bird find out that sitting in the middle of an ant's nest was a good idea because the formic acid produced by ant bites (or is it stings?) kills feather mites. Genes are bound to be involved somewhere, of course, but we're discussing the *first* bird, the one that made the discovery, before any genetic patterns were established.

This all arose because, while stuck in the school traffic on my way to work one morning, I gave serious consideration to the scientific name for the spider who lives in my wing mirror. I've unofficially dubbed him, or her (how do you sex spiders unless you see them both together?) Eugene, but, on reflection, Neugene might be more appropriate.

Neugene has lived in the fat plastic wing mirror of my car for as long as I can remember. He has travelled considerable distances, witnessed – in my absence – a sprinkling of parking fines and is fully aware of who it was that wrecked my rear off-side reflector panel and didn't stop!

Neugene has survived car washes, although there have been times when I've washed the car myself rather that write off a brand new web. He has travelled at high speed on motorways, suffered electronic adjustments and his home has, on occasion, been clouted by other wing mirror spider residences while negotiating Jersey's more narrow country byways.

The Ford Company knew what they were doing when they stuffed their cars into wind tunnels. Neugene's web can handle speeds of up to 75mph – no problem! On the other hand, Ford web efficiency equals under-nourishment too because even Neugene balks at fielding a hover-fly travelling at 75 mph. This led me to the conclusion that Neugene feeds when the vehicle is stationary. All good scientific stuff!

One final thought on the matter of Neugene and his high speed web. Pied wagtails have the habit of attacking wing mirrors and all kinds of reasons have been suggested. Mine, for what it's worth is that they, the wagtails, are after Neugene and vanity or pugnacity don't even enter the frame. Well, it's something else to reflect on.

Painted Lady

Map of Jersey showing main areas of natural habitat and other places mentioned in the text

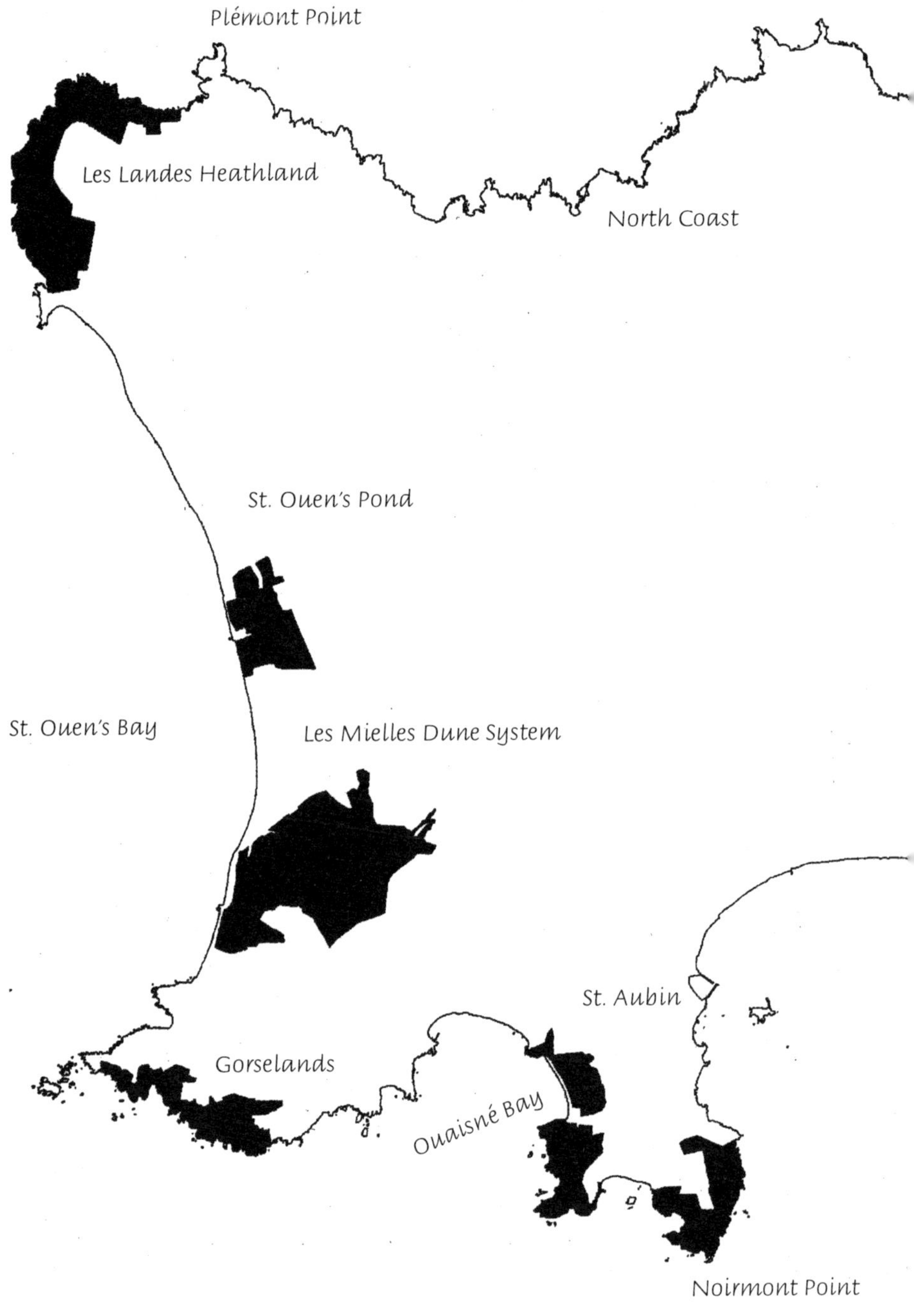

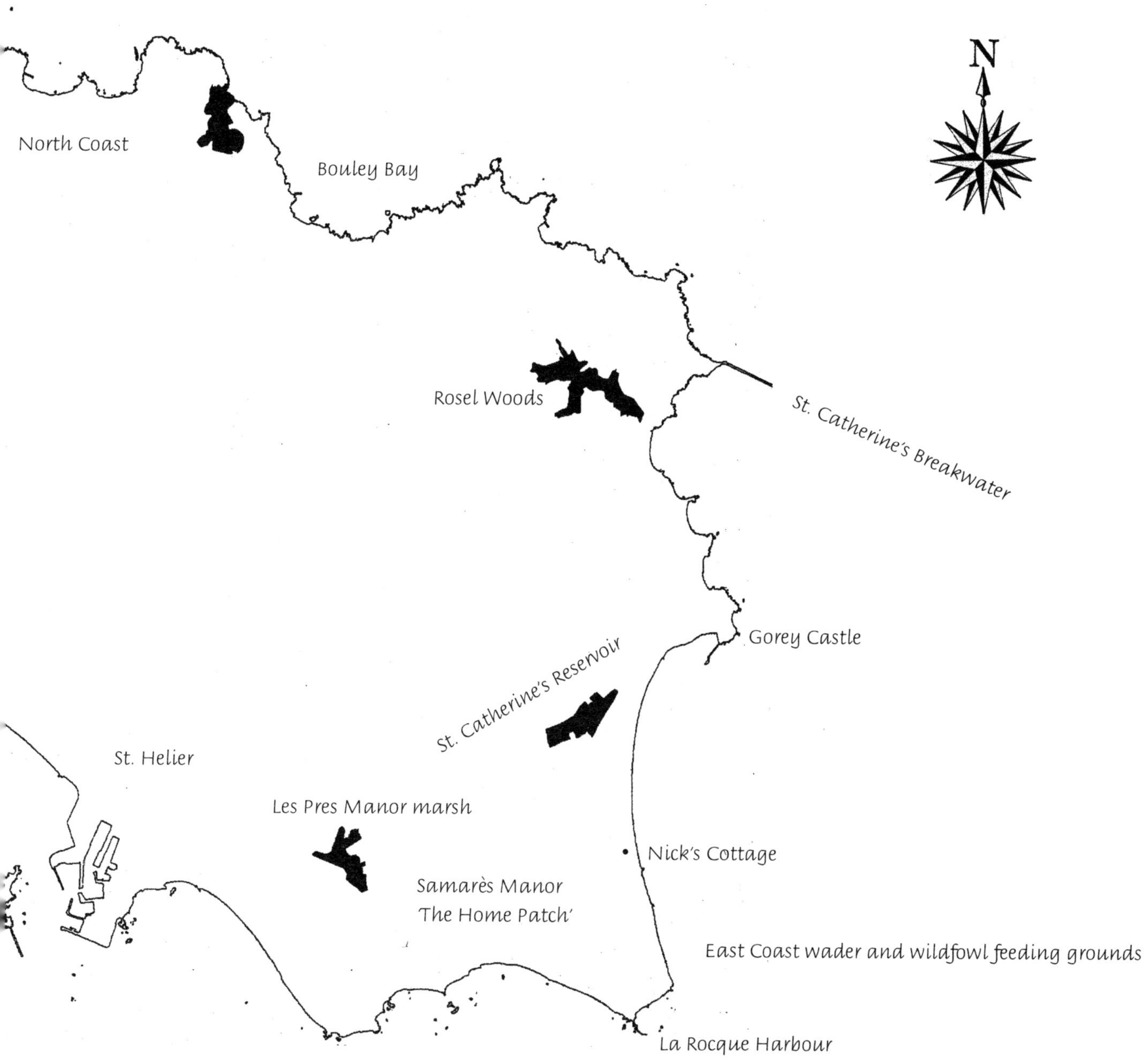

N
North Coast
Bouley Bay
Rosel Woods
St. Catherine's Breakwater
Gorey Castle
St. Catherine's Reservoir
St. Helier
Les Pres Manor marsh
Nick's Cottage
Samarès Manor
'The Home Patch'
East Coast wader and wildfowl feeding grounds
La Rocque Harbour

JULY

A GLOWING DAY-TIME HEAT made gorse pods snap and gave the brassy sun an uninhibited chance to achieve melt-down. The air is filled with insect sound and the boringly repetitive song of a cock chaffinch is becoming seriously irritating to everyone but his well hidden mate.

The weather is getting to that point where Islanders and holidaymakers have had enough sun for a while and the general consensus of opinion is 'we need a bit of rain to clear the air' – classic symptoms of a weather-conscious race living on and above the 50th parallel. The French think we're mad of course. Ask a Breton what the weather's going to do tomorrow and he gives you that down-turn of the mouth and a lift of the shoulders that says, 'Who cares'.

Despite the heat, the evenings are glorious. I love that brief period when the swifts and a handfull of swallows and house martins don't quite know when to turn in and the bats, flitting between the limes, would prefer just a little less light. Henry Williamson, or at least I think it was H.W., called the time 'dimmit light'. It's a very short, magical moment, like the peak of a handsome sunset. It's a stag beetle time too. Giants among their kind, they clatter through the dusk, like noisy hang gliders and, as the wind drops, other, lesser insects, rise through their own avian efforts much to the delight of pipistrelle bats seen in silhouette against an orange and lemon sky on the verge of becoming night.

Pipistrelle hunting

I spent my annual fortnight in Brittany and, as usual, managed to add copious notes to my nature diary. I make observations and later enjoy comparing details with the Island's natural world. This year's notes, the ones with the five stars and several exclamation marks, announce that I've seen my first ever real live fox. Not one of those suburban foxes causing such a stir among the dustbins of England, but a real rural type.

I was standing at the edge of a wood about eight kilometres from the town of Lamballe in Brittany quietly bird-watching. There was a narrow tarmac road running alongside the thick canopy and opposite the wood were open fields. I'd parked at the entrance to a dirt farm track and was casually resting against the bonnet of the car just listening to the early morning bird song. It was just after 7 a.m.

First Fox

The fox simply walked around a bend in the road about forty yards away. Low sun backlit the animal beautifully and finally, when 'Monsieur Renard' realised I was there, he, or was it she, stood stock still, huge ears pointing in my direction and then, in a flash, the glimpse was a memory.

Looking back now, assisted by notes I made at the time, the animal was not as sleek as I would have expected. Not like those 1940s story books which were inclined to give the fox a coat like a red setter. It had an almost woolly appearance, as if the winter coat had still to fall and the mask was exactly right, featuring those small black marks on either side of the lower jaw that remind me of black teeth. Another clear memory was that he *was* gloriously red – not brown, ginger or rust but a lovely rich red. And I can still remember being totally amazed by the size of the ears. In volume they were much bigger than the head.

There were foxes in Jersey during the eighteen hundreds and, much like the bird species recorded at the time, foxes had to be shot to be believed. I suspect powder and shot were cheaper and more readily available than photographic equipment in the second half of that century and the general view, even to naturalists, was that a shot specimen was proof;

a sighting, mere hearsay.

At some point they were introduced to the Island and over a period of about twenty-five years bred successfully in the country parishes. What was thought to be the last fox was killed in St. Brelade in 1870.

I don't think I'd like to see foxes in Jersey again, as appealingly romantic as the thought may seem. They would probably make inroads into the cliff-dwelling bird populations, especially the shags and fulmars and eventually they would become bin bag robbers and subsequently lose their appeal *and* their dignity.

I recorded starlings roosting in reed beds in France and was surprised to discover on my return that a high percentage of the Island's starling population, between twenty and thirty thousand birds, have been using the reed beds at St. Ouen's Pond as a roost for several years, which, in turn, shows how much time I spend at St. Ouen's Pond at dusk in autumn.

The return trip to Jersey, aboard the car ferry, *Solidor II*, added a final and delightful milestone to the holiday. With Seymour Tower on Jersey's east coast over to starboard and the Minquiers reef looking like a row of battle ships in the haze to port we were joined by a party of sun-flashing, exuberant, bottle-nosed dolphins.

Although my eyes were glued to binoculars most of the time I was constantly aware of the delight these gleaming acrobats caused among the passengers. The bar emptied, and even restaurant lunches went briefly unattended.

Bottle-nosed Dolphin

What is it about dolphins that attracts us so much? Perhaps it's that curve of the mouth that suggests they have a sense of humour. Maybe it's not humour. Perhaps it's a knowing look, a look that hides a secret that we have yet to earn the right to understand. These animals were fat, healthy and a wonderful sight to behold; their appearance just off the Jersey coast put smiles on everyone's faces. I think that's what dolphins are for.

Perimeters Perceived

It's a hot, clear evening in mid-July and from my vantage point, overlooking the meadows, below the house, there's every indication that nature is more aware of the predicted, hot dry spell, than us.

From where I'm sitting I can see paired-off soldier beetles on every thistle and yarrow flower head. Between the tractor ruts around the edge of the bean crop, fat hen, mayweed, the rusty heads of broad-leafed dock, redshank and scarlet pimpernel have all managed to avoid the plough. That thin strip of wild flora that survived the pre-planting preparations is some indication of what the rest of the meadow might have looked like had it been left to lie fallow. Splashing the dust-smooth tracks with continental colour are at least half a dozen painted lady butterflies and at my feet, hundreds of heavy-weight, winged ants are wandering about trying to decide what to do next.

I knew earlier in the day that the ants were on the wing, swarming into the world with little or no control over their destiny. There was a great pyramid of black-headed gulls over St. Helier. The flock stretched two or three thousand feet into the afternoon sky harvesting the hapless insects being lifted by the warm thermals. Out-flying, out-manoeuvring and out-feeding the gulls and making them look like a squadron of cumbersome heavy bombers, swifts cut through their noisy ranks like Harrier jets, bearly visible in the upper air.

Two meadows away a couple of herons spiralled down on hollowed wings like parachutists to join others at the traditional La Blinerie roost. The scrub oaks at the roost look as though someone's whiter-than-white washing has blown away and snagged in the branches. The little egrets are back in numbers.

Only four egrets used the La Blinerie roost during June, the other hundred or so headed south into Brittany and Spain, some to breed and, I suspect, there were non-breeding birds too, just tagging along for the ride. I counted forty-six birds on the 14th of July and by the 25th there were fifty-four.

Heather and Heath

Les Landes, the long stretch of heathland on the north-west coast, is unbelievably beautiful at the moment. It is awash with the deepest, richest hued flowering heather and the sound of a dozen species of bees, plying their trade among the billions of flower heads, is almost soporific in its intensity.

The contrasts between heather, the low, buttercup-yellow, western gorse and the blue of the sea at Les Landes in July is positively stunning. Add to this a huge sky, uncluttered but for a cruising cloud or two, and any feeling of confinement on a small island is simply lost in space. Since cars were banned from the heathland tracks at Les Landes the dusty roads have begun to narrow. Heather, scented mayweed, bugloss, scarlet pimpernel and cranesbill are all helping turn tracks into footpaths.

The cliff-top paths cut through the heather for several miles, past Gronez Castle and on towards Grève de Lecq. It's a good place for stonechats and, later in the year, peregrine falcons can often be seen, possibly because the cliffs are home to quite a large population of stock doves. At the moment Les Landes is in its most gentle mood. A place for skylark and meadow pipit, butterflies and insects and colour, such colour!

Inter-Tidal Trek

On the other side of the Island the shallow sea is warming to the summer sun. Nick and I waded, ankle-deep, across the low tide shore and watched mullet and bass scatter as we approached. Every tiny pool is alive with fish and, taking the coast as a whole, there must be literally billions of fry that could only have hatched this month. When the tide is out the shallow pools, even those puddles between sand ridges, contain fish. The sand becomes warm and, as the tide begins its journey up to the splash zone, it in turn is heated by the sand, creating the perfect incubator for eggs and an ideal nursery ground for the fry.

The bass, of course, even six-inch fish, are predators right down to their tail fins and what is a nursery to fry is a larder for small second-year bass, hunting in packs. On a calm day the presence of bass in the shallows is signalled by smaller fish leaping clear of the water among the weed-fringed low tide reefs in a bid to avoid becoming a meal.

There are hundreds of thousands of mullet inshore too. They feed on molluscs, diatoms and worms and as Nick and I waded through small gullies we could see them rolling and glinting in no more that six or seven inches of water a few yards ahead.

With more than two-thirds of July already gone we were not altogether surprised to see curlew feeding at the water's edge but a party of dunlin in summer plumage and a couple of turnstones *were* somewhat unexpected and we saw at least one redshank flying low along the waveless water line. Further out to sea there were common terns plunging into the water on every hand, their excited cries, supported by the ratchetty grating sound of sandwich terns, suggested a successful breeding season on the off-shore reefs.

The seashore is just beginning its own very special kind of metamorphosis. Subtle changes are taking place. The sea has grown warm. New sounds are beginning to fill the hushed summer air. There will come a time soon when the constant, not-a-moment-to-lose movement of thousands of waders and their calls will fill the air with piping excitement and the low key mood of this middle month will be lost for another year.

However, at the moment there are few audible distractions. Nick and I are standing waist-deep in a gently rising sea with just water sounds for company. All around us mullet are disturbing the smooth surface – not feeding, not going anywhere in particular, just enjoying the sun and lazing about like holidaymakers.

A Tight Line at Seymour

The bass we are after are much less demonstrative and have no intention of giving us any indication of their whereabouts. Well not, that is, until one of our small, hardly noticeable floats switches and slides off at a ferocious pace into the calm clear depths, giving the lie to this outward picture of tranquillity.

It's good rod-bending stuff but the bass, all prickle-finned and warm to the touch, are small and are returned to the water. Apart from our lugworm, they are feeding mostly on the huge clouds of whitebait which have been drifting aimlessly past us for some time. Next month the fry will have the mackerel to contend with as well as greater numbers of terns. Whitebait really do live on the edge.

Pupa Scooper

You know how confusing it can be, trying to identify a moth. Well it's even worse trying to pin a name to a caterpillar. Last winter I transferred some small, healthy great mullein plants from the Manor rockeries to my wild garden. Apart from the bright yellow blooms they produce I quite like the texture of the leaves and the tall strong look of the plants.

The lower leaves of my great mullien suddenly developed holes. A diligent search produced one of those stranger-than-fiction caterpillars with more colours than a supermarket shelf. Many caterpillars are inclined to look alike to me so 'several thumbs through the book' later I was more confused than when I started. Then I had a brainwave. *Look up mullein in the moth section,* and there it was: Mullein Moth. Since then I've determined that the name of the plant will sometimes lead to the name of the caterpillar. I know that might seem childishly logical to you, dear reader, but it was like discovering that hover-flies really are flies, to me.

It's been a good year for kestrels. Every nest I know has produced young, and along the Five Mile Road on the west of the Island they can be seen hovering as evenly spaced and almost as numerous as telegraph poles at times. These small, fierce little falcons can be seen in every habitat in the Island. They've nested at La Pulente quarry, St. Catherine's Wood, in the Colombière at Samarès Manor and at La Moye this year, to my knowledge, and doubtless in farm buildings and coastal cliffs all over the Island.

Sparrowhawks are a different kettle of feathers though, I haven't seen any since the winter. There are at least a half dozen pairs breeding in the Island, which, considering there were no birds resident in the Island at all during late 1950s and throughout the 60s, is encouraging. They are rather a secretive bird at the best of times and I suspect the glimpses we do get are mostly during that leafless time of year when they seem to widen their hunting areas considerably. At the moment, Jersey's thickly wooded valleys provide them with food and plenty of cover, so they manage to keep a fairly low profile.

A Make-Shift Muscovy

Most of the resident wildfowl are going through their annual moult at the moment and the drake mallard are looking particularly drab. The term describing this lack-lustre period is called eclipse and I'm not quite sure why. They do spend a lot of time mooning about but I'm sure that's not the explanation. Muscovy ducks, on the other hand, are still as handsome as ever. I know they're not regarded as particularly serious birds from the twitcher's point of view but I have a particularly soft spot for them based on an experience which occured during my Scottish sojourn. This is how it happened.

Once a course angler, always a course angler, I suppose. I had been thrashing the River Orkey with a worn-out Dunkeld for about an hour. It was blowing a bit of a 'hooley' from the west and the noisy rough and tumble of the river's rills and onward flight to the quieter waters of Loch Awe, along with the wind in the trees, had pushed my thoughts inward; a

A Fine Old Bird

float fished lobworm kept was becoming a serious consideration. It was while I was immersed, at least mentally, in the sheer heresy of considering fishing the 'garden fly' on a traditionally sacred Scottish trout and salmon stream that the Muscovy duck made its waddling appearance on the other side of the river.

He was a fine old bird, all iridescent feathers, gnarled and knobbly about the bill, a penetrating red eye and a carefully considered gait which brought him to the edge of the Orkey moments after the demise of my fly, which, apparently, preferred the succour of a mature alder to the whiplash of my back cast.

The gale was blowing upstream and the only reason I was there instead of pike fishing by Kilchurn Castle was simply that Loch Awe is twenty-four miles long and with the wind coming in from the west, the loch had a surf running so making it impossible to fish. But the upstream blow seemed to suit the Muscovy because, with hardly a pause, he dipped his rounded breast into the current and shoved off.

Now you'd have thought that, despite the wind, the bird would have been whisked quickly downstream in a series of undignified spins, bobs and swoops. Not a bit of it! To my absolute astonishment this Muscovy lifted the primary feathers of his left wing into the strong breeze and casually sailed a broad reach over from his side of the river to mine. A thorough shuffle of the feathers later, he continued, with unaffected nonchalance, up the bank and out of sight.

I sat on a moss-covered rock amidst the din of wind and water, rolled a cigarette and considered what I'd just witnessed and concluded that animals don't have the ability to reason – apart from Muscovy ducks that is. I've had a great respect for them ever since.

July closed hot and crisp and August looked as though it could well compound the situation. Little rain, gleeful holidaymakers and more butterflies than I've ever seen before. The colour is beginning to drain out of the summer canvas although, thanks to a wonderfully wet late winter and early spring, headlands, coastal walks and heathlands are surviving the summer with consummate ease.

A Gorse Spike

AUGUST

A WEEK INTO THIS LAST month of summer and spring tides are dropping down to that rarely observed zone in which marine plants and animals, not normally subjected to shallow water, provide a fascinating source of interest for anyone with an ounce of curiosity and a prawning net.

As Nick and I made our way over the hard-ridged sand, legs constantly splashed by cockle fountains, a flight of grey plovers flew in from the sea, birds, I suspect, freshly arrived from the tundra of northern Siberia. Not the dowdy, unspectacular grey birds of winter shorelines but birds still in full and glorious breeding plumage. Silver-spangled crowns and backs separated from jet black breasts and bellies by a narrow band of snowy white. They looked gorgeous! The colours fade quite quickly once they settle into their wintering routine but this early glimpse is such a seasonal delight.

When we finally reached the tide line, a good mile from the land, it took a hundred yards of wading to reach knee-deep water. Over the white sand, the sea was a most delicate blue-green, the kind of colour seen reflected through Arctic icebergs in fine weather. Above forests of kelp around the reefs, pin-sized sand-eels, almost matching the colour of the sea, swam just ahead of us. This beautifully sun-bathed vision was accompanied by the sound of terns, their wings back-lit, their breasts providing the only white in an otherwise cloudless sky.

Nick climbed to the summit of a rocky out-crop and cast a bait into the still water. I hunted for anything interesting at its base. There was very little movement on the surface, which was unusual for such perfect conditions, until suddenly a heavy disturbance about forty yards out ridged the water and explained the reason for the lack of fish movement.

"Mullet?" I asked, assuming Nick had a better view.

"Not unless mullet take very deep breaths," he replied, at which point a bull grey seal broke the surface and eyed us suspiciously for several seconds.

Grey Plover in Summer Plumage

A Grey Seal broke the surface

I still don't know whether standing up to my waste in a kelp bed with a two hundred pound bull seal swimming in the vicinity is a good thing. For a moment or two the prawning net felt a bit inadequate but the pleasure of having seen him at all was the high point of a great afternoon and we decided later that the headline MAN BITTEN BY SEAL WHILE PRAWNING was one not often seen in newspapers.

Summer Wings

There are butterflies everywhere, drunk on nectar and windfall fruits. They are even turning up on the beach. Tortoiseshells in particular seem to find something attractive about the beach and the rocky outcrops at the edge of the tide.

On one buddleia bush during a filming session, I found I could put a finger on the blossom and these beautiful insects would just climb aboard. The predominant garden species are peacocks, red admirals, tortoiseshells and speckled woods with an occasional comma or clouded yellow turning up from time to time. I actually filmed a buddleia blossom with four species feeding on its nectar all at once.

A local newspaper report announced that thousands of red admiral pupae have been found in a country parish field where previously caterpillars had demolished a couple of acres of nettles. When they fly, the sight should be quite remarkable.

There also appears to be something highly attractive to wasps and red admirals exuding from the base of an oak tree near home. I suspect its

Buddleia and Peacock

sap although it looks a bit like the froth on a pint of real ale. At times the lower trunk is covered with wing-flashing admirals, each insect dipping its long hollow proboscis into the sap and drinking. They're big butterflies and the constant opening and snapping shut of the wings as they fed warned off the competition very effectively. I was interested to note that the motion was used to repel wasps. The rapid wing movement was enough to knock these slow-moving insects sideways when they approached too close. The admirals only moved off when the wasps ganged up and invaded the feeding area in numbers, five or six at a time. Looking through the lens I got the distinct impression that the wasps' strategy was co-ordinated.

On the north coast cliff walks, common and holly blues, wall-browns, meadow browns and small coppers are a common sight among the sea campion, scabius and heather. On these walks the views are stunning in the fine weather and with a mixture of greater and lesser black-backed gulls, herring gulls and fulmars soaring over the landscape, the feeling of space and freedom is truly exhilarating.

Sadly, the swifts have gone. A sure sign, toward the end of the summer, that the month has passed its zenith. The swifts are the last summer visitors to arrive and the first to go. There will still be more northerly birds passing through for a while but I shall miss the way they scream over the town, chasing each other's tails. They nest annually in both Fort Regent and Gorey Castle and it seems sad to think that the comparative quiet following their departure will last for another eight months.

And talking about Gorey Castle, I've always felt that that stately pile, overlooking France and dominating the east coast, would provide the scene for a wonderful natural history television programme. Officially, the Castle is unoccupied but that's not really true. Kestrels nest there every year, in some areas wall lizards allow visitors to pass within a few feet of their sunbathing ledges between the granite blocks and, when the lamp houses floodlight the battlements at night, they attract a huge variety of moths, some very rare indeed.

It's interesting to consider that perhaps the same wild flowers found on the castle's steep slopes today have been seen for a thousand years

by sentries standing guard on windswept walls. And there's no reason not to suppose that endless generations of swifts have chased above the heads of countless attackers and defenders throughout history. I wonder sometimes if the rats I see working the tide line beneath the walls of Gorey harbour could be the ancestors of those which enjoyed the inevitable refuse created by British Redcoats, French infantry and the steel-helmeted troops of the Third Reich. Food for thought, if you'll forgive the pun.

Hawkers and Darters

Don't you just love dragonflies? Nature's version of the helicopter I always think. I only give them any thought when I see them, in late summer, but they've been quite prolific this year so I decided to delve a little more deeply into the history of these aerodynamic glitter-bugs.

Emperor Dragonfly

Dragonflies haven't changed much for a hundred million years, not since the Carboniferous Period when coal seams were forests. They must have shrunk in size a bit because when they roamed swampy forests stretching from Canada to Western Europe one species, at least, carried a wing-span of seventy centimetres, about the same as a herring gull. Wow!

I've seen several species this year including emperor and gold-ringed, plenty of common blue damselflies too but a couple of sightings left me scratching my head. I saw one – a brown, broad-bodied specimen, on the edge of the cliffs at Les Landes and a couple of brownish-red darters on the escarpment above L'Etacq. I'm not bold enough to put names to them of course although it would be a bit easier if they'd just stay still for a moment.

The emperor is a wonderful beast. It's the largest of the British dragonflies – full of aggression and all action. I watched one at St. Ouen's Pond from one of the fishing platforms recently, patrolling his patch in the calm water sheltered from the wind by thick reed beds. When a small warbler flew from the sedge out into the open I was amazed to see the dragonfly actually chase the bird back into cover, and since then I've watched another escort a swallow off his patch when the bird had the temerity to grab a drink while on the wing.

Questions I used to ask myself about dragonflies when I was a youngster were, I suppose, standard. How long do they live? Do they hibernate? How far do they travel? Do they sting? I add this last question because my reference book fails to mention that bees, wasps and horseflies *do,* so who am I to assume that dragonflies *don't.* I won't answer the questions now, dear reader, treat this as your special project.

One of the penalties we pay for prolonged hot spells is the high risk of furze fires. One has raged all day today above Bouley Bay and was only brought under control after much effort over difficult terrain. There's no doubt that the aftermath of these summer blazes looks awful but if there's going to be such a fire, far better it happens in August than in May and June when the bird breeding season is in full spate. I find it curious just how often a cigarette end is blamed for these conflagrations. I wonder how they started before cigarettes were invented ?

The steep headlands will recover. The renewed growth, for a while at least, will provide open areas for other wild plants and, when the gorse does establish itself again and the dense smoke and flames are but a memory, the new low cover will be perfect for Dartford warblers, stonechats and linnets. It should be interesting to watch the area develop.

On my way to work this morning I counted over a hundred little egrets at the roost. The job was made easier by a lack of wind and the birds choosing to perch on the sunny side of the scrub oaks to preen. As I made a note of the numbers, the radio announced more hot weather to come, so I decided to put some time aside for a fishing trip at the weekend while the fine weather lasted in this final month before autumn.

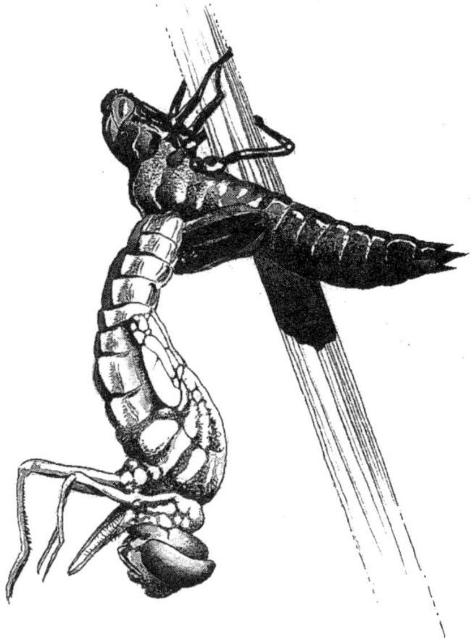

Metamorphosis

Tight Lines

My favourite summer fish is the garfish, a long-nosed, green-boned pugnacious character with a jaw full of fine, needle-sharp teeth and, pound for pound, one of the best fighting fish in the sea.

The spot was one of my favourites. The climb up would be a pipe-opener, but that would be later. Right now, the weather was good, those long foamy patches, created by the sea pounding the un-submissive rocks at the base of the cliffs, was sliding down the tide in white ribbons. There was a very definite smell of garfish in the air.

Looking down the steep slope with its rocky outcrops, soaked in bright yellow lichen, the shimmer of summer-fat herring gulls and green carpets of succulent hottentot fig gave me great pleasure and a feeling of pleasant anticipation. The tide was rising; all the familiar components of a good garfish session were there and, as far as I was concerned, all was right with the world.

On the lip of the steeply sloping cliff face, sea campion and patches of heather added

Oystercatchers

colour to the pink hues of granite and, to make the picture complete, echoing up from the lower cliffs came the sound of oystercatchers. I've found their nests often enough while lowering myself carefully down to these unfrequented fishing marks; that moment when the eye focuses in and the brain says 'you are looking at three very well camouflaged eggs on a very exposed rock' never fails to give me a thrill.

Here and there are signs which suggest I'm not the only one who knows about this place. An aluminium ring pull, a rusty hook or two and a coloured bead wedged in a crevice are clues, but today, apart from an agitated rock pipit and a species of fly that, without fail, homes in on my bait container as soon as I arrive, this precarious perch is all mine.

The tackle is standard stuff for garfish – ultra-fine line, a light carp rod, a pencil-thin float and a number six tinned hook. The bait is a thin strip of last year's garfish designed to look as much like a sand-eel as possible and, because garfish are mid-water and surface-feeding fish, the bait is set to drift about ten feet below the surface.

The first cast sails out into the tide and the float settles perfectly just at the edge of a strip of foam drifting by some thirty yards away. Every angler will tell you, and it's not just an old wives' tale, that garfish love to hunt under and jump over things. Patches of floating seaweed and driftwood are an enormous attraction to these eel-slim silver fish and it's not surprising really because they are truly oceanic surface feeders. Their prey is most likely to congregate in areas which afford a bit of protection from predators.

The float tilts its way down the tide and swings into the edge of a foamy drift where the contact with sea and rock has charged the water with oxygen. It's a good place for small fry to be and the garfish know it.

Just offshore a passing crabber catches my attention. The boat has its mandatory flock of herring gulls in tow but, with the pots fishing and old baits gone by the board, their chances of a meal is unlikely. While I watched the boat my float took a dive. But the nice thing about garfish is that it's not a good idea to strike too soon. Sometimes a lapse of concentration can be useful.

I stood up, tightened the line and leaned gently into the fish by lifting the point of the rod without actually striking. The result was a very satisfying curve in the carbon fibre and a powerful dead stop at the business end. No chance to retrieve line at this moment. Just keep up the pressure until the fish decides what to do next.

It's the stuff angling is made of. The fish breaks the surface twenty or thirty yards out, leaps high into the air, plunges back and dives deep. A few minutes later the spent fish is lifted out of the water and the smell and feel of emerald green scales drying on the fingers as you eat a well deserved sandwich is an experience few will enjoy.

A little later, a sprig of tarragon, a splash of white wine, seasoning and chunks of garfish simmering in foil on the barbecue completes the day. The meal is a bonus but being below those cliffs on the south-west coast at peace with the world was the true *raison d'être.*

The Spot was one of my Favourites

Tree Nesting House Sparrows

Sparrow Speculation

There's a tree growing down at the manor, well, more tall shrub really, with lanceolate leaves serrated into spines, and, hidden within each separated group of leaves is a single, very tough, and very sharp thorn. Foreign, definitely, but nevertheless it's festooned with half-a-dozen, haystack-sized house sparrow nests. I referred to my reference guide, because I considered house sparrows nesting in trees quite unusual, only to discover that they nest in the eves of houses *and* in hedges. The text makes no suggestion that it's unusual but I reckon if I asked a dozen bird-watchers how many house sparrows' nests they'd found in hedges during their travels, the answer would err on the side of none. In my opinion it's a pretty unusual sight to see so many nests in a single tree.

The numbers of house sparrows in Britain is estimated at many millions, which points to a very successful species indeed. So much so that given a little sunshine in January they will go into breeding mode.

Judging by the appearance of the nests, which seem to get larger every time I look at them, I think they just keep adding to the original nest which probably started off as a small service flat and will doubtless end up with four bedrooms *en suite.* I do like house sparrows. They're tough, no nonsense birds and the poet, Norman MacCaig, captured the essence of the species in his poem 'Sparrow.' The poem always makes me chuckle, especially the second verse which sums up the bird's character perfectly:

To stalk solitary lawns,
to sing solitary in midnight trees,
to glide solitary over grey Atlantics –
not for him: he'd rather have
a punch-up in a gutter.

August is looking a bit tired after the effort of giving us such splendid weather and there are definite signs that summer is in retreat. It's only the faintest suggestion of change. Trees have a slightly weather-worn look about them and the gathering of house martins and swallows, in the air and on overhead lines, reflects more than just a successful breeding season.

The sounds of waders on the tide line is becoming increasingly noticeable, the bright red berries of lords and ladies are beginning to show beneath heavily laden hedgerow elders and, although it might seem normal to fungi experts, I'm beginning to cast an eye for mushrooms. I think all it will take is a little rain to encourage my favourites to show themselves and, with the Florida hurricane season pushing change our way, I don't think it will be long. Even now a strong westerly blow is chasing grey cloud in from the Atlantic but the sky seems reluctant to shed its load on this parched Island.

Knowing the Drill

The pebble-dash facing on Nick's bungalow has several tiny circular holes in it. When I say tiny I mean less that an eighth of an inch across. Nick pointed them out to me during a quiet *aprés fishing* cup of tea. He'd seen wasps disappearing into the holes from time to time and kept an eye on them. Using a dead stamen of a nearby geranium (Nick had got a little behind with his 'dead heading'), he teased the entrance to one of the holes and a small larva made its appearance at the entrance.

Later I checked out the possibilities regarding this cave-dwelling infant and came to the conclusion that it was the offspring of a mason wasp. Apparently there are nineteen species of mason wasp found in Britain. They make a nest in the loose cement between bricks, fill it with a paralysed caterpillar and add an egg. The larva develops using the caterpillar as food. You see, it's not necessary to hunt the Island for nature in the raw. It's happening right there in the brick-work. All you have to do is sit and watch.

SEPTEMBER

IT'S EASY TO GET A bit 'prosy' about September – mist, mellow fruitfulness and all that – and I make no bones about experiencing a certain sense of loss when the month eases in. The farewells of summer still echo everywhere. Dragonflies continue to cruise pond margins; moths still flicker through car headlamps; trees stand fully dressed and individual starlings remain content with their own company. I think the feeling of nostalgia is rooted in the fact that we realise subconciously that this pretence of a seemingly unending summer won't last.

For me, the essence of September has always been the smell of apples and blackberries – it's the perfume of a summer well spent. The month is snared by a profusion of sun-lit cobwebs, showered by goldfinch-floated thistledown and laden with uncertainty.

If I'm lucky, there's a momentary glimpse of a vagrant honey buzzard, a mere speck in the afternoon sky. There's always an intrusion of leggy craneflies (daddy longlegs if you prefer) to look forward to, casting shadows from beneath living room lampshades. It's a month designed to ease us gently out of the warm embrace of summer and into change.

From now until mid-October birds are at their most prolific. The summer residents are still here, apart from the swifts, that is, and the wintering species are arriving in droves. It's eight months since that January bird watch so I think it's time soon to do it again, while wintering arrivals, passage migrants and the after-guard of summer residents are still here. It should make an interesting list.

Reef Encounter

Yesterday I purposefully marooned myself on the Casquets reef for a whole day with nothing but a camera for company. Seven miles west of Alderney, the place has an atmosphere all its own and, visually at least, it could be almost any time of year. You really have to look closely for seasonal clues on the Casquets. When I was there, the only sounds were the sea and the voices of herring gulls bouncing off granite. Apart from the briefest glimpse of a solitary blackbird, which in itself was peculiar, nothing else stirred.

The Casquets, with its now automatic lighthouse, can be an unnerving place if you're in the wrong frame of mind. The day I clambered onto the main reef, trying desperately to keep my barefoot balance on a mat of dark green slime covering a cracked and crumbling slipway, the sea was outwardly calm but there was an underlying menace in the smooth, racing water. It was hot and humid and I'd forgotten to include a drink with my filming equipment. By the end of the day I'd experienced the merest hint of what it might be like to suffer from thirst.

Wild Island

I was there on that lonely out-post to record the place where, ninety-five years before, the reef was the scene of the worst tragedy in Channel Islands maritime history. Seventy-seven people died one cold March evening when the London and South Western Railways steamer, *Stella*, crashed over a reef, yards from the lighthouse rocks, at eighteen knots.

The death of the *Stella* was easy enough to picture. There was thick fog at the time, freezing cold conditions and, because of the sound of the sea and the mighty blast of the fog horn, the lighthouse keepers heard nothing. She sank within ten minutes of striking, a kilometre away from the reef, amid the treacherous overfalls off Alderney. It was almost dark and leaping into such turbulent waters, with only a cork life-jacket, must have been a terrible experience for those Victorian sea travellers.

Sea Mallow

Perhaps because of its extraordinary loneliness, the Casquets is a perfect place for small birds to rest during autumn migration. The only plants remotely resembling bushes are the thick, fleshy-stemmed sea mallows, tucked into rocky crevices and sheltered from the prevailing wind. How they manage to find sustenance in such inhospitable surroundings is hard to imagine.

Bird-watchers lucky enough to have spent short periods there in company with the duty lighthouse keepers, have recorded up to seven species of small songbirds in a single mallow, so sparse are the roosts on the reef.

A Successful Wild Goose Chase

It was a Sunday afternoon. There was a mixture of cloud and intermittent sun overhead and the traffic was heavier than usual. The lights turned green at the end of Fort Regent tunnel and, as I followed the slow moving procession through the underpass and out onto Victoria Avenue, I had ample time to reflect on the likely success of my mission.

I was chasing the rumour that a lady in St. Brelade's regularly fed red squirrels by hand. By the time I'd negotiated the log-jam at the end of the Avenue I'd convinced myself that even a hint of truth in such an unlikely story was worth investigation, especially considering how little footage I had of Jersey's most delightful and elusive mammal.

In the back of the car, along with my video paraphernalia, was a hide. I'd worked on the assumption that such a nervous animal might find my presence a little disconcerting although, frankly, by the time I had circumnavigated the bends of La Haule Hill and begun the climb towards the top of Pont Marquet I was far from optimistic about the outcome.

The lady in question is Abigail Corcoran and when I arrived at her small, tree-shaded bungalow perched above the brow of Pont Marquet Hill, there was a van parked outside the door. She was in the throws of moving house.

"Ah! You've come about the squirrels," she said, mop and bucket in hand. "I've put some food our for them. They should be along any time now. You won't mind if I get on, the house has to be empty by tomorrow morning." Abigail disappeared into the house just as the television came out.

Across the gravel drive there was a small lawn planted with broad-leafed trees. On the grass beneath them were several dishes filled with a mixture of sunflower seeds, broken digestive biscuits and fruit. At the far edge of the lawn was a chain link fence and, beyond that, some twenty feet below the level of the garden, was the main road.

I set up the camera and waited half-an-hour. The removal van was almost full when Abigail appeared once more.

"Any sign of them yet?" Her confidence was awe-inspiring considering the fact that we were talking about a rare and supposedly timid animal.

"Well, no, not yet. I was wondering, perhaps, whether I should set up the hide. Maybe I'm putting them off."

"Well you can if you like, although they don't usually mind strangers."

At least sitting in the hide made me feel as if I was attempting to be serious. Another half-hour passed. Apart from the removal van crunching off down the drive, nothing stirred.

"Hello! I've brought you a cup of tea." I clambered sheepishly out of the hide and accepted the tea with the thought that Sir David Attenborough never got cups of tea and two Marie biscuits when he was waiting for lowland gorillas.

"They really are naughty you know. I think I'll call them. Give 'em a bit of encouragement." I bet Sir David's intrepid guide never said *that* either.

Abigail walked over to the chain-link fence and in a loud, semi-operatic voice, shouted, "Come on! Come on! Come on!" And then, as she headed back to the traumas and stress of moving house, added, "There, that should do it. Just keep an eye on the woods and you should see them start heading this way."

The van came back. The driver clambered down from the cab and asked me if I'd seen them yet. My shake of the head brought a puzzled look to his face. "That's odd ! They were all round my feet yesterday. I was worried I might tread on one."

Wild Island

Just as I thinking this whole situation could be a serious wind-up, I saw them. Two at first, flitting from bough to bough through the woods on the far side of the road. They seemed to be converging on a point where an oak overhung the road and joined forces with a false acacia at the end of the garden. It was a perfectly safe, high-level bridge.

The first squirrel appeared in the garden, upside down and stretched across the lower trunk of a young sycamore looking as though it was stuck there by suction pads. From where I stood there seemed to be no visible means of support on the smooth bark. A brief pause, presumably to judge the distance, and suddenly the creature was sitting upright on the top of a flat bird table contentedly making inroads into a piece of biscuit. The leap was about five feet and the speed was incredible. Just a blur of movement and a hyperactive, glossy coated red squirrel was sitting six feet from where I stood, totally unconcerned by my presence.

A Friend of Abigail's

I counted four squirrels that afternoon and there was a definite pecking order during their activity at the feeding station. Their colour varied quite considerably – red, certainly, but on one in particular, the dominant member of the party, I think, the back and tail carried an almost mink-black lustre.

The leader of the group took several pieces of biscuit from Abigail's finger-tips and two took advantage of a water bowl lying on the grass. There was another with only one ear, which suggests that the life of a squirrel is not all a bed of hazel nuts.

It was a fascinating experience and the footage I gathered takes pride of place in my collection. Abigail, who seemed to take the whole thing in her stride, had managed to gain the confidence of those animals to an extraordinary degree. I just hope the new residents on Pont Marquet hill enjoy the same success.

Subway Supposition

The front page of the *Daily Telegraph* caught my eye this morning. Commuting bird-watchers had reported feral pigeons using the London Underground as a means of getting across the capital. According to the report the sightings even warranted a piece in the *New Scientist.*

Apparently, birds have been seen quite regularly joining the rush hour populace on the Piccadilly and Bakerloo lines and the suggestion is that they really do know where they're going. I don't think so! Any bird that can get from one end of Regent Street to the other in the time it takes a taxi to stop at the lights would hardly attempt a subterranean route. If there is truth in the rumour, however, it would seem that the passenger pigeon, a species thought to have been lost for ever, like the dodo, is not extinct after all.

I have seen birds use public transport on occasion. During an autumn sea crossing to France I was once joined on the after deck of the good ship *Solidor II* by half a dozen swallows who took advantage of the ship's direction and the flat surface of the lifejacket boxes to preen and rest. The ship was ploughing through a rather misty afternoon on its way to St. Malo. The mid-crossing respite appeared to suit the birds fine. They stayed for about twenty minutes before continuing their journey. I have to confess though that there was no sign of feral pigeons on board, either on the car deck or the bridge.

Pole Position

I'd been filming small copper butterflies in a field lined with well established tamarisk on the west coast. Weighed down with a tripod, camera, batteries and a field guide, I emerged from the entrance and came face to face with what looked like a polecat. It had all the right markings and was sitting on a pile of fine sand at the entrance to a large rabbit hole, which is probably the most likely place to see one.

Above: Flocking Ferals;
Below: North Coast Bandit

I think it was a recent escapee because it was quite content to let me unload all my equipment and set up the camera before deciding to slip quickly into the rabbit hole. It was an hour and a half before the animal decided to re-emerge. It tested the breeze with a diligent nose and considered its surroundings with extreme care. It was twenty yards further away from where it had originally dived for cover which showed just how honeycombed with tunnels the rough ground is at Les Mielles.

More by luck than judgement I was downwind and the animal, with only its head showing above ground level, allowed me to film it.

Polecats and ferrets are not indigenous to Jersey but escapees are, according to some naturalists, having a diverse effect on the Island's wildlife. It's quite possible that they and other predators are the reason why the puffins on the Island's north-western cliffs never seem to increase measurably, despite ideal conditions.

I'm sure there's a very close connection between the success rate of certain cliff-breeding birds and the presence of ground predators and I had an opportunity to make the comparison during a visit to Skomer, an island off the south-west coast of Wales.

Skomer is the traditional breeding ground for about forty-five percent of the world's Manx shearwater population (around one hundred and sixty thousand pairs) and there are some six thousand pairs of puffins. Both are burrow-nesting species highly susceptible to predation and, if one works on the basis of one egg or fledgling per nest the total number, including adults, is round the half million mark. Amazingly there are no ground predators on Skomer.

Somehow Skomer has managed to remain free of weasels, rats, cats, ferrets, polecats and the like although there was a panic on one occasion at a time when the island's farm was still a working enterprise. A rat was seen leaping ashore while a cargo of hay was being unloaded. It took four days of continuous baiting to trap the animal and, when it was eventually caught, close examination showed it to be a gravid female.

North Coast Puffins

Jersey, on the other hand, does have its fair share of domestic, feral and wild ground predators – polecats and ferrets in particular. Islanders use them of course to hunt rabbits and there are bound to be losses. It's worth noting too that a considerable number of the Island's agricultural labour force is temporary and while they work here some use polecats and ferrets to hunt rabbits for recreation and for the pot. It's been suggested that some of the animals are released into the wild when their owners leave the Island.

At least thirty polecats and ferrets were trapped in a single summer on the north coast by a naturalist who wanted to prove a point. Puffins would be an ideal target as a food source, eggs or young, especially as they regularly use old rabbit holes as nest sites and the terrain on that coast provides perfect cover for the covert activities of the weasel family. It's quite possible too that the introduction of such predators into the Island, whether accidentally or otherwise, could well be a contributing factor to the depletion of green lizard and agile frog stocks.

The Closing Bars

Rain and high winds at the end of this month have finally brought down the curtain on a memorable summer though even now, when the sun breaks through, it's still T-shirt warm and the tarmac tends to steam a little.

On fine days the sun lights the hawthorns, their crimson berries adding a richness to the colours of autumn; then, suddenly, as these roadside hedges begin to lose their leaves, all the bird nests you missed during the spring are revealed.

The local mallard, out of their drab, almost embarrassing moult, are flying with great exuberance past my den window – glad, I suppose, to be buffeted by a clean wind and free from the ties of land. Their tight formations, with a back-drop of sun-lit *cumulus nimbus,* remind me of a Peter Scott painting.

Mallard free from moult

OCTOBER

Above: Black Nightshade
Below: Redshank

THE MIDDLE MONTH OF AUTUMN. Not, it would seem, the most inspiring of months, if the great poets are any kind of bench mark, and I find that surprising. It's odd that those writers who have chosen to write about specific autumn months should neglect the one which produces the most colour, the most fruit and certainly the most visible signs of change. Perhaps they couldn't think of anything to rhyme with October!

So far the month is quiet and unruffled. The sunsets are glorious, the early mornings drenched with dew; and the apples, a few yards from my den window, have sunburned to a glowing mixture of colours which reflect perfectly the role this month plays in the Jersey calendar.

In fairness to the poets though, the flora does seem to come under the sub-heading 'inconspicuous.' A casual patrol at the edge of my meadow in deliciously warm sunshine produced redshank, the only plant making any effort to create colour. I found the small white flowers of black nightshade – that lover of waysides and, as Nick pointed out, a member of the potato family (not a lot of people know that). Shepherd's purse was there, fat hen too and just a few heads of yarrow were still in bloom.

Nothing much there to motivate creative prose but take heart, this month is no less enjoyable than any other, despite being abandoned by the bards. In my opinion, it's brimming over with as much treasure as Palgrave's fifth edition.

Orbital Observations

Even now there is an abundance of insect life working the hedgerows and the number of fat orb web spiders squatting in the centres of their beautifully constructed snares is quite remarkable. Among their captured prey I've noted carder bees, moths, ladybirds, craneflies and even small caterpillars although I suspect the latter were accidental entrapments.

The orb web spiders are extraordinary engineers. One specimen in my garden has managed to build a web above an eight foot privet hedge and the main anchor cable is at least five feet higher, attached to the very corner eve of the house. So how is the gap spanned ? I think he, or she, must have streamed the silk out on the gentlest of October breezes allowing it to tangle in the hedge and, once the connection was made, the rest was simple, for a spider anyway.

My bird table has four posts supporting the corners of its roof and there are five or six spiders working the space in between. When the sun catches the intricate pattern of webs it reveals a dozen or so beautifully constructed traps all of which overlap, making it almost impossible for a careless insect to avoid the sticky silken maze.

Hedgerow Hunter

I saw a spotted flycatcher taking advantage of the October sun late this afternoon. They do nest here in summer but I got the distinct impression that this was a bird passing through the Island. Just a brief respite in order to stock up energy for the long haul south. Its general appearance of buffs, browns, creamy margined feathers and the streaked, rather than spotted, pale breast, makes it an unpretentious bird and yet its skill as a hunter of insects is pure poetry in motion.

My bird's vantage point was the weathered arm of a dead elm set among the tough thorns of a fruit-laden briar hedge. Through binoculars I could see the bird's head turning in complete circles as it followed the flights of a variety of potential targets. It chose a wasp – drunk, I suspect, on fermented blackberry juice. With the precision of a master, the flycatcher left its perch, took the wasp in mid-flight and returned to the elm.

A flick of the bill removed the sting and the wasp was no more.

Spotted Flycatcher

In Praise of Ivy

Much of this late insect activity coincides with the flowering of ivy in the Island. The plant may be a vexed question in some circles but in my view it plays an integral role in nature. To begin with, it's not a parasitic plant. It sends down roots and finds sustenance in the ground just like any other tree or shrub. When ivy does climb trees the trunks merely act as climbing frames and, from my own experience its presence, whether in woodlands, waysides, old quarries or sea cliff faces, appears to be an essential part of the ecology of those habitats.

The ivy in my garden is mixed generously with brambles and sycamore saplings. Its flowers are attracting wasps, hover-flies, speckled wood, red admiral and holly blue butterflies to say nothing of wrens and gold crests. It's an evergreen of course and its thick foliage provides shelter for many species of insects as well as acting as a roost for the smaller birds.

In spring, ivy attracts nesting birds. Among my notes I've recorded wren, robin, blackbird, song thrush, spotted flycatcher, tree creeper, wood pigeon and jay, all hiding eggs in its thick cover and, according to recent observations, the red squirrel finds the dry shelter of ivy foliage much to its liking too. Occasionally, ivy will dominate a tree and at such times the weight of snow or rain water on the leaves could have a diverse effect on the supporting host but, as long as woodland trees are managed carefully, ivy is no real threat.

Ivy provides a ground-covering evergreen in woodlands and valleys and produces succulent black berries in winter. The fruit attracts all the thrush family including Jersey's huge winter population of redwings and fieldfares. It also provides my very favourite resident songster – the blackcap – with a regular source of food and for that, I am truly grateful.

Ticking Truants

Why is it that bird-watching during the working week always manages to touch my conscience. The feeling probably stems from a mis-spent youth when, on fine summer mornings, I'd find myself bird-nesting or fishing instead of applying my mind to school lessons and carrying out my duties as ink monitor.

Jersey, despite being a comparatively small Island, still offers areas where solitude can be found but many of the Island's best bird-viewing platforms are well within sight or sound of a hard-working populace.

On Friday the thirteenth, Nick and I were standing at La Rocque point listing species for that promised autumn bird watch. In the background we could hear the commuter traffic grumbling its way into St. Helier for another day of faxes, phone calls and inter-office politics. I entered bar-tailed godwit in my note book while experiencing a delicious sense of isolation, a feeling of actually standing outside the *real* world. And there it was, just the smallest pang of guilt. Typical of the effect forty-five miles of coast can have on the range of bird habitats, La Rocque produced all the usual waders and sea birds but added magpie, pied wagtail, meadow pipit, carrion crow and kingfisher, which demonstrates just how many of the indigenous species regard the shoreline as a regular source of food.

The sea appeared to have been freshly ironed. A haze hid the horizon and the off-shore rocks, cobbled with cormorant, oystercatcher and curlew, seemed to hang unsupported in the morning light and for once, thanks to a calm morning, La Rocque was quite warm.

At Le Pres Manor, several oak trees edge the narrow lane overlooking the marsh and, because the day was perfectly still, a tiny shower of water droplets from the crown of one of them attracted Nick's attention. The tightly bunched yellowing leaves had apparently collected tiny pools of dew overnight, and taking full advantage of them was a bluetit. The bird had discovered a high-rise bathing pool. As each collection of water was emptied by rapid wing beats, the bird moved to the next water-filled cluster. That's what I love about nature – it is continually showing us something new.

Wild Island

By the time we reached the west coast the sky was cloudless and the temperature was up in the low twenties. The bird report book in the St. Ouen's Pond hide had now gone into hardback. The upgraded book, we decided, was just a more sophisticated means of informing us that we'd missed black tern, bittern and gadwall. Nevertheless, our list was already up in the high fifties so we could afford to be a little sanguine about missing a few birds passing through.

One bird we decided not to chase was the cream-coloured courser which had been sighted and photographed in fields near Hougue Bie. It's the first of its kind to have been recorded in the Island since 1896 and far more eminent 'birders' than us had made the identification reliable.

Although the bird was on our doorstep it doesn't appear on my tick list. I rarely chase after rarities. I think it's because I consider common birds more fascinating than those which occasionally lose their sense of direction or have to take whatever orientation a heavy gale chooses to set them. Somehow, the 'twitcher's tick,' as fulfilling as it may be to the twitcher, is so remote from the realities of true bird-watching that I'd rather discover a bluetit bathing in the crown of an oak tree than travel a thousand miles to tick a fantailed warbler on Fair Isle. It's a personal view of course.

In the heat of a remarkably fine day our bird watch stuck at sixty-two species. From it, we learned that there were very few house martins in the Island; that the fulmars were noticeable by their absence on the north coast and that the winter build-up of pied wagtails had begun.

We missed treecreeper, spotted flycatcher, bullfinch and great spotted woodpecker but discovered that nine little egrets had chosen the poplars at Le Pres Manor marsh in preference to the overcrowding at the La Blinerie roost. My most recent count of these 'northern settlers' is an incredible one hundred and forty-four.

The day after our Island tour we added greenshank, sandwich tern and house martin to the list which, on a good day, could have easily reached eighty plus. As it was, we were perfectly content with sixty-five species over the twenty-four hour period.

Road Runners

Driving a car around Jersey is not the best way to enjoy the Island's natural history. Being encapsulated in steel, glass, plastic and man-made fibre tends to be a bit disorientating. It

Something moved across the road

seems to me that the time between the start of a journey and its end is mostly lost in a series of kaleidoscopic images which the brain discards almost as soon as the journey is completed. Occasionally, however, moments seen through the toughened glass of the windscreen do stay, especially if you're the kind of driver who nature watches *en route.*

Frankly, it's not a recommended pastime unless you happen to be a passenger and even then, shouting 'barn owl' at the top of your voice just as the car is negotiating a notoriously dangerous bend in the dark, tends to make the non-naturalist driver lose concentration.

I've circumnavigated hedgehogs, narrowly missed wood mice, avoided magpies, dodged toads and I've even carried out a speed test on a wood pigeon that just happened to be flying a parallel course to my car. All pretty normal events for a nature-loving motorist but the most bizarre road runner I've so far encountered led me to believe I was in no fit state to be driving at all.

It happened while I was on the way to Nick's bungalow for the beginning of that most recent bird watch. The road was clear as I traversed the bends of St. Clement's inner road and crossed the parish boundary into Grouville. Ahead, something moved across the road from left to right. At first I thought it was a leaf – after all, it was October. Then I realised it was a bit too steady for a leaf and anyway, there was no wind. As I flashed past I got the distinct impression I'd just seen a rather large green crab.

I'd barely touched a drop the night before and yet *green crab* remained uppermost in my mind. As I slowed down at a particularly narrow piece of road on that Friday morning it suddenly occurred to me that I'd been following a trail of old seaweed, dotted about the road in tufts, for about half a mile. It was then that thoughts of *delirium tremens* began to fade.

October is *vraic*-gathering time on Jersey beaches. The great piles of seaweed loosened from offshore rocks during gales is swept up the beach with spring tides and local farmers gather it by the lorry load. It's a fine, natural manure and what warms the hearts of Jersey farmers even more is that it's free. The unfortunate crab must have been picked up in a pile of weed as the harvest was being gathered and later parted company with the tractor trailer before it reached its destination.

I *did* go back, but I couldn't find it.

Parish Perambulation

There's one parish walk in particular which gives me great pleasure. It covers the sea-shore, marshland, common land, rural countryside, a thick fringe of hedgerows, well established allotments and even a wooded escarpment. I always begin on the concrete apron which runs in a north-easterly direction along the seashore from Le Hurel slipway to the first tee on Grouville golf course. Half tide up or down at this time of year will produce mixed flocks of sanderling and dunlin, grey and ringed plover and the raucous conversations of Brent geese.

On the golf course proper a pathway follows the sea wall, passing through tall stands of fennel. Directly ahead the sweep of the Royal Bay of Grouville ends beneath the battlements of Mont Orgueil Castle. It's a good place to see flocks of green finches at this time of year and, in early spring, wheatears bounce over the close-cut fairways hunting flies. Cirl buntings find the open spaces to their liking and nest in the thick patches of gorse but, sadly, the carefully manicured terrain, once a common, is no longer honoured by the cadences of skylarks.

Just before the square-cut granite of Fort William I usually cut north-west across the fairways past Jersey Potteries and on to the higher ground along La Rue du Moulin de Bas. There are well established allotments on the right below a wooded escarpment and on the left the terrain overlooks a small bird reserve. The reserve is filled with a mixture of sedge, willow and oak and is actually part of the marshland leading on to Le Pres Manor. The flat marshy area floods during winter and attracts teal, widgeon, shoveller and snipe. The road which passes the entrance to the Manor eventually leads back to the entrance to Grouville golf course which almost brings me full circle.

It's the variety of habitat which makes the walk so absorbing and it's best enjoyed in late spring or October when the trees are not too well dressed and passage migrants make nice additions to the resident bird list. My best ever bird count on this route was sixty-seven species. The distance around the circuit is between three and four miles.

Starling Performance

It's nearing the end of the month. The clocks have been meddled with so the light is now dying at around five each evening but, despite the lime trees in the grounds of the town church looking somewhat forlorn, they've been given a new lease of life. It's starling time and thousands upon thousands of birds have replaced the trees' autumn foliage. Their murmuring is like an umbrella of sound which pervades the noise of home-going traffic and the sight of undulating flocks arriving from all points of the compass in the clear October sky is positively breathtaking.

Because this October has been among the most gentle for years the starling flocks have chosen other roosts as well as the more traditional sites. At the moment, for example, there's a bright yellow crane dominating the St. Helier skyline on the east side of the town. Every evening the hard lattice-work of girders is softened by row upon row of fidgeting birds when the perching spaces are filled to capacity. Other circling flocks move on to search out alternative accommodation. This massive autumn gathering is in such contrast to their summer existence when they are much less sociable birds, preferring the individual family unit to the shoulder-to-shoulder crush of cold weather crowds.

At dawn each morning they leave the roosts in marauding bands to feed on farmland – especially around cow sheds where cattle are wintering – heathlands, parks and gardens. There's nothing subtle about starlings. They don't feed at garden bird stations, they raid them, dominating the bird table until all the bulkier food is cleared and then they'll even hang on the nut baskets pretending to be blue-tits, but at this time of year there's an abundance of windfall fruit, worms, insects and berries to sustain their numbers.

Starling time

It's estimated that there are between four and seven million pairs of starling in Britain and, considering that in 1880 they were only a winter visitor in Jersey, the species appears to have been remarkably successful.

They're wonderful mimics and have fooled me dozens of times with perfect renditions of curlew, redshank and grey plover calls. Whether they pick these sounds up while feeding on the piles of winter *vraic* around the coast or the copycat songs are brought by the Scandinavian birds which join forces with the local population in autumn I'm not sure, but I welcome their company and enjoy their repertoire immensely.

A Mullet Well Met

The wind has swung around to the east and is bitingly cold. The land temperature has dropped but the sea is still comparatively warm. The high tides are rolling old weed up the beach and behind it, in the disturbed water, mullet show flashing bars of silver as they feed on fly larvae in the shallows.

I baited up with a small piece of fresh bread and let the swell carry the float where it would. They're an odd species the mullet. One moment they can be tantilisingly timid and the next suicidally audacious, but until you set a bait among them you can never tell which mood they're in.

The wind was picking up and my fingers, for the first time in months, were frozen. Above the land an enormous moon was lifting out of the haze, turning from a grey wash to gold as it picked up the light from a setting sun lighting the sky behind me.

I was fishing at the Dicq by Havre Des Pas. Water surged over the jetty and drove me up onto the rocky outcrop below the White Horse Inn. Out of reach of a sea that seemed restless and indecisive in its direction, I watched the tip of the float slide from crest to crest until, without preamble, it dipped beneath the surface.

The mullet, a grey mullet, was about two pounds in weight. As it slid over the rim of the landing net the last rays of the sun caught its flank and bounced gold and silver shards off the armour plating scales. The fish was in perfect condition and it still is. I slipped it back into the water and, with numbed fingers, packed up the gear and headed for the car.

The very last vestiges of summer had gone and it was good to say thank you.

NOVEMBER

WHILE SHUFFLING THROUGH THE LEAVES beneath a plain tree that's trying in vain to keep its foliage on board, it's easy enough to conclude that this is a dead month. It probably means you've got your head down, shoulders hunched and are counting the shopping days to Christmas. If that's the case, you'll doubtless miss the first string of visiting lapwings loping across the skyline above and the vole threading its way through the chestnut roots exposed under the bank on the far side of the lane.

Observation is the key to making this month as enjoyable as the rest and, from this naturalist's point of view, there's a need to fill every month with notes of change in order to make the year complete.

This morning, head up, my breath proceeding me down the lane in a steamy cloud, I decided the low temperature wouldn't last. There was far too much weather activity out in the Atlantic for a cold snap like this to continue.

Under the hedges among broken nettle bones, frost laced the edges of dead leaves and picked out the patterns of cobwebs sagging with the weight of ice particles. The sun, which earlier warmed Africa, was snared in brittle hawthorns; the great orange disc turned chuckling redwings into sooty black silhouettes as they moved among the late berries.

Through a granite-pillared gate a field filled with healthy looking cauliflowers climbed in regimented rows up the hill until the orderly ranks merged into the blue shades of distance. Their leaves were studded with sparkling pearls of water which gave the crop an even richer texture in the early morning light. On the road ahead a spent rocket underlined the time of year (November 6th).

Goldfinches, more a hyperactive troop than a charm, had gathered in this last month of autumn to glean the seeds from a withered summer. Crowds of gold-barred, red-cheeked finches fell from the hawthorns ahead and onto the margin of a field still bright with the remains of an exhausted tomato crop.

Lapwings

Birds are most likely to attract the attention at this time of year. Not simply because they are more easily seen among the bare boughs of autumn but because the days are short and the nights are long and food becomes an all-consuming priority.

The period of stillness and quiet which occurs during the day in the middle months, when many birds rest and leave the duties of natural sound to insects, is past. Although there is more food available now than in spring, there is far less time to gather it, hence the constant activity.

Spider Loophole Plugged

Even the most wily outdoor type can occasionally be trapped by the demands of domesticity; after that early morning walk I found myself, paint-brush in hand, clean out of excuses and confronted by a bathroom in dire need of a lick of paint. For once the pleas of a glib-tongued amateur naturalist failed to cut the proverbial ice.

I flipped the lid off the pot of silk emulsion with the tip of a screwdriver and watched it roll across the bathroom floor, only to land sticky side down on the bath mat. I decided I had been out-foxed by a spouse with a mission, and got on with the job. As I retrieved

Opposite: Redwings at sunrise;
Right: Goldfinches and teasel

the lid I checked the bath from whence I'd carried out many a spider rescuing operation time past. I remembered how I'd once tried to put a friend's mind at rest regarding the dreaded 'spider in the bath' myth.

She was totally convinced that the plug hole in her bath and the overflow aperture further up comprised the lair of unspeakably large, hairy spiders, which occasionally got caught napping when she turned on the bathroom light.

I indulgently proffered what I was convinced was a rational argument by pointing out that when she did find them in the bath they never ran away. Then I trotted out a bit of the old logic.

There's a mystical world of pipes, ball cocks and T-joints called plumbing connected to the bath and one of the most important items in the system, apart from the ubiquitous bib and brace, is a thing called a U-bend. This sophisticated piece of apparatus is always filled with water and, unless the spiders in her bath had undergone a course in sub-aqua techniques, there was no way that they could get into the bath via the plumbing.

I expected a look of enlightenment but, instead, the frown deepened as I went on to explain that the bath was actually a giant spider trap and that highly polished, smooth fibreglass and enamel surfaces were, for spiders, impossible to climb. Once the spider falls in, unless his mates lowered a rope he's in there until you walk in and wash him clockwise down the plug-hole from which he or she never emerged in the first place.

I didn't think it possible that a frown could deepen any further, especially in the face of such simple logic, but it did.

All her life she'd been thinking, for plug-hole, read spider's den. All my explanation did was put the whole thing in a completely different and far more sinister light. If they didn't come up through the bath, where did they come from?

In the long run it would have been better had I said nothing. The comfort of assuming that spiders live down the plug-hole and all rush up to the overflow for refuge when she let out the water, was gone. Now, instead of trying to make pictures out of the patterns in the cushion flooring, she apparently spends her time checking out the recesses, the badly fitting joints in the wainscoting and the gap behind the bathroom cabinet. At least with the bath scenario she could keep an eye on things – a sort of focal point for spider activity. Now, she's never sure and can't stand naturalists.

I wiped a smear of emulsion off the bathroom mirror and got on with the job.

Some like it hot

I was stuck in Weymouth with a full gale blowing and no chance – according to the shipping forecast – of getting back to Jersey for at least a couple of days. That, in the middle of November, with rain lashing in from the south-west, might seem a depressing situation, but I was undaunted. In fact I was rather pleased.

The car was full of camera equipment along with a couple of spare tapes; right in the middle of Weymouth is an RSPB reserve. My cup, once again, overflowed.

The links between Weymouth and the Channel Islands go back centuries but it is surprising just how few Islanders are aware of the wildlife the town has to offer.

Radipole Bird Reserve, just a couple of minutes walk from the town centre, is like an oasis. There are paths cut through hundreds of acres of reed beds interlaced by fresh water channels. In some areas the water levels are controlled to provide scrapes – sheets of water which make ideal feeding grounds for visiting waders. At first glance these stretches of water could be ten feet deep with cloud reflections hiding their true depths. Then suddenly a snipe or common sandpiper will nip over the sedge and begin feeding with feet hardly covered.

In addition, there are wide expanses of water where, in early summer, slab-sided bream roll on a surface teeming with bird life.

At Radipole you'll never get closer to great-crested grebe, coot and ruddy duck and, on half-drowned, wind-polished poles, placed there for that very purpose, cormorants stand phoenix-like, drying plumage and digesting fish.

I lugged the camera gear into a hide smelling of freshly applied creosote, opened the observation shutters and waited for something to happen. The sound of a moorhen calling from the reeds below the hide was accompanied by rain beating on the roof and, to add to the general cacophony, an incoming flight of tufted ducks swung into the wind, skidded neatly onto the water a few yards away, and began discussing the flight in muted tones.

Cormorant drying out

I'd been in the hide for about half-an-hour when a cormorant drifted into sight. The bird was low in the water and was accompanied by a very agitated freshwater eel of some two pounds in weight. There then began the most fascinating battle between a bird bent on lunch and a fish determined not to provide it.

The cormorant managed to swallow the eel five times but on each occasion left the very tip of the fish's tail protruding from its bill. Slowly and inexorably the eel re-emerged, hit the water and the chase began all over again. I never did see the result of the struggle because the cormorant, with head held high and neck convulsing in a variety of shapes, finally disappeared from view.

As I trudged back towards the car beneath lowering grey skies and diminishing light, the eel-versus-cormorant affair got me thinking ... imagine floating in the middle of a lake in the pouring rain in November and lunch, in this case an eel with a mind of its own, keeps regurgitating itself.

"Eat it while it's hot." How many times has your ever-loving mother voiced that time-honoured gem at the dining table? Yet we're the only species on earth that considers hot food essential. I suppose the larger carnivores might argue the point but, from my own observations of those television documentaries featuring 'gratuitous wildlife', lions only 'eat it while it's hot' because if they don't they probably won't get any. I wonder what would happen if the human race never ate another hot meal ?

Pied Spied

I was down among the sodium lamps of night-time St. Helier harbour looking at the fishing prospects when nature decided to introduce me to one of its countless secrets.

At the top end of the harbour complex there's been a yacht marina for a number of years and, moored beyond the safety of its half-tide wall, are a mixture of gin palaces and serious boats. The wall, which separates them from the lifeboat mooring and the general activities of a busy commercial harbour, is built with huge interlocking blocks of sand-coloured stone.

Rain was drifting through the yellow glare of the lights as I made my way along the New North Quay to a point where the blocks stretch out across the harbour. For some reason the great stones are not flush-edged as one might expect but bevelled where they meet; this forms a continuous ledge between each row. Roosting on the ledges were at least six or seven hundred pied wagtails. Row after row of birds filled the deep-cut joints. Occasionally, a bird would make a restless flight up through the rain-swept lamplight and back to a crowded shelf. Others were sleeping, heads tucked beneath wings, on the floating pontoons where, close by, boats rocked gently to the wind passing through the bare poles and stays of winter rigging.

I was delighted with my find. No doubt others knew of their presence but it's so gratifying to make the discovery unaided. It just goes to prove that, no matter where you are and at what time of day, Nature will always grab an opportunity to show you just how little you know.

I took Nick down to the harbour a couple of nights later in pretty much the same weather conditions and they were all there, flitting and fidgeting under the sodium lamps.

All he kept saying was, "Ah, bless 'em!"

Every time I see pied wagtails now, whether on the beach, in the middle of town or beside pools in flooded fields, I think of the St. Helier Harbour roost, its constant light and the halyards rattling a discordant cacophony on the top of the tide as a hard gale pounds over the Albert Pier from the west.

That's not much to look forward to after a hard day's fly catching but, if you're a wagtail, I suppose its home.

"Ah, bless 'em!"

A Flock of Birders

There were Barbours, windcheaters, dufflecoats and even the odd Burberry down at La Rocque Point last Sunday. It was a sort of corporate bird-watch and, despite a chill Force 4 blowing in from the west, the sky was clear and the mood very sociable amongst some seventy bird-watchers strung out along the granite harbour wall.

The nice thing about a bunch of birders, if that's the collective term, is that no matter which way you decide to look, someone else is looking in the direction from which some wayward ornithological gem will appear.

Take the swallow for instance. There I was, focusing on a couple of purple sandpipers glued to the leeward side of an offshore rock when up went the cry 'swallow'. Don't be daft, I thought, it's November 26th.' But it was indeed a swallow and, in retrospect, I should have realised there was bound to be one delinquent wondering where the rest of the gang had gone. I told you swallows were a bit dim!

Then there was the kingfisher, skimming low across a confused swell below the sea wall. By the time everyone was pointing in the right direction the bird was long gone. For once I'd been pointing in the right direction.

When the call went up for snow bunting I suspected it was given by one of the few people there who had the nerve to put a name to it. Albino linnet might have passed through the odd mental list too but, as it happened, it really was a snow bunting – a female, taking advantage of newly sown grass seed on a sloping bank facing the sea.

When the wind is in the west at La Rocque there are some beautifully protected areas below the sea wall and, if the sun happens to be shining in late November, there is inevitably some fly activity. This was confirmed by the appearance of a female black redstart, a pair of stonechats, numerous rock pipits and several pied wagtails.

To seaward there was a raft of about a hundred red-breasted mergansers. Later the birds broke up into small groups and, with the sea quite rough off-shore, the less experienced among the binocular-bedecked gathering always manage to search for mergansers when the swell places them neatly in the trough of a wave. The remark, "No, they're Brent geese," seemed to be the phrase of the day.

Snow Bunting Female

Red-Breasted Merganser

At one point I braved the wind and spray in order to check out a flock of curlews homing in on a reef besieged by white foam. There was a photographer from the local paper eyeing the situation from beneath the shelter of a high granite buttress. I strolled over to the safety rail, picking my way between the clumps of seaweed and pebbles, and stood for a few moments, watching the birds tentatively parascending onto the reef.

Wild Island

"Tide seems to have dropped a bit now," I observed, knowing full well I had no idea whether it was coming in or going out. "It should be safe enough to take a few shots from here."

The *crump* of a wave hitting the base of the pier was the first indication I had that it wasn't safe at all. I turned from observing a flock of dunlin catching the sun in frantic flight to see the photographer extremely wet, regarding a camera which appeared to have been dunked in a bucket of sea water.

With as much aplomb as I could muster, I handed him a couple of used tissues and melted into the crowd just around the corner. It was with some relief that I viewed a picture of curlews roosting on an offshore rock in the *Jersey Evening Post* the following evening.

The snow bunting proved to be the most tolerant bird of the day. With watchers arriving throughout the morning there seemed to be an unspoken agreement that the crowd would keep its distance in order to give late arrivals the chance to view a bird that had, until recently, enjoyed the environs of the Arctic tundra.

It was only when a family party of mum, dad, three youngsters and a push-chair passed within ten yards of the bird that I realised just how tolerant these birds were to human beings. I dashed for the car and a little later captured some delightful snow bunting shots.

Closing Bars

There are old apples littering the ground beneath the tree and I no longer have to step warily to avoid wasps. Their nest – deep amongst the hardening stems of fennel in my wild patch – is silent. No more clumsy insects emerge from the dark recess that, for months during the summer, I had carefully left unsmoked and free from the automatic reactions of less tolerant gardeners. I'm still not quite sure for what purpose wasps were placed on this earth but I personally have no grudge against them and if spotted flycatchers consider them an ecological necessity, that's good enough for me.

This eleventh month has proved a little more difficult to record than I had anticipated. Throughout its uncertain moods I've been conscious of the fact that November is predominantly a bird month, but then avian activity is so bound up with this season of change that it's impossible to ignore the presence of birds.

Withering by winter, hibernation by winter, the lowering of the metabolic rate by winter are natural processes which render November a lean month. But, whatever Nature is up to, the birds are aware of it, they take advantage of it and they, of all species, are the naturalists to watch. They really are the guide to discovering Nature's natural progression at this time of year.

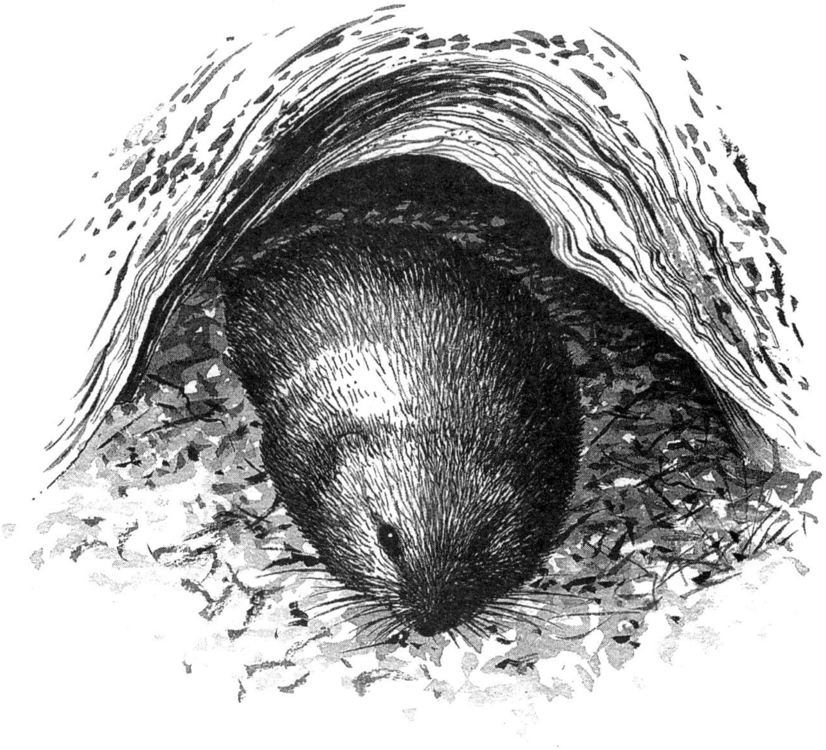

Bank Vole

DECEMBER

Above: Hawthorn;
Opposite
Top: Snipe;
Centre: Widgeon;
Bottom: Teal

At first, December seemed somewhat reluctant to admit it was a winter month. The temperature climbed into double figures and then, after an encouraging start, the rains came and so did the fog. The hawthorns along the lanes of the high parishes were dripping with moisture and above the north coast cliffs the familiar sight of headlands sliding into the sea simply had to be imagined.

Then it snowed. Just a light icing sugar dusting but enough to tell me there were rabbits in the brambles at the far end of my wild patch. The elongated prints of hind feet with a couple of forepaw dabs told a very clear story and yet I'd seen no sign of them previously. It was a happy discovery. I need all the help I can get in keeping that wild patch under control. When the skies cleared the frost came. Most of the wetland areas were fixed with a wafer-thin coating of ice, leaving widgeon, teal and snipe little to do but wait for shadows to shorten and hope for an indolent sun to send a modicum of warmth into their feeding grounds.

And talking about the wild patch, the month has replaced the leaves on my apple tree with a goodly mixture of finches, house sparrows, collared doves and tits. The bird table stands directly beneath the tree. Within a couple of hours of rigging up the winter feeding station and distributing largesse in the form of peanuts and sunflower seeds, a disorderly queue had formed and considerable inroads were being made into the offering.

The redwings and fieldfares have pretty much laid waste the autumn berry harvest and are now concentrating on the Island's pastures and meadows. There are thrushes everywhere. I counted no less than five species while searching the area from the comfort of my double-glazed den.

Song thrushes and blackbirds worked the wheel-rutted perimeter of the meadow, leaving mistle-thrush, redwing and fieldfares to attack the worm population on the broader expanse.

Wild Island

The ivy is laden with fruit in various stages of ripening and two or three hundred lapwings are sculpting aerial patterns over freshly ploughed fields.

I'm not quite sure why the wintering lapwings fly with such exuberance. One minute they are content to blend in amongst the furrows and the next, they lift off and draw shapes in the sky. Possibly it may be in order to create body heat or perhaps one of the local kestrels is causing corporate nervousness. I like to think, not very scientifically, I know, that they actually enjoy these impromptu air displays.

Hair of the Dog

Several cracks appeared in a sky which, for days, has had the appearance of cold porridge. So, on this Saturday morning, armed with a pair of pruning shears, I brought the buddleia hedge under control with a will, gave the pear trees a short back and sides, cut the scratchy teasel heads down to ground level and then stood considering the apple tree.

There's a blue-tit nesting box pinned to one of the more solid branches. The box, which is painted green with a fine moss at this time of year, becomes active at about the same time as the bee-crowded apple blossom is at its best.

It didn't take much mental persuasion to convince me that there wasn't really enough daylight left to tackle the tree. I decided to clear out the nest box instead.

Now I have the good fortune to be owned by a golden retriever who is as daft as a brush and, very often, twice as smelly. He lives, sleeps and breathes retrieving, although he's never heard a shotgun fired in anger at close quarters. He allows himself to be bullied by our two home-grown cats but shows the less tolerant side of his nature when it comes to the non home-grown variety.

Bird Dog

Apart from testing the agility other people's feline pets, he has an ongoing dispute with the local magpie population over the biscuit he invariably leaves overnight in his food bowl. The magpies rattle the stainless steel dish at sun-up every morning and, naturally, he gets rattled too. But little does he know it's not just the magpies who covet his biscuit mix.

I came home late one night to discover a very large hedgehog standing four-square in the bowl devouring the leftovers. Judging by the noise it was making while munching its way through the meal, I was convinced the old chap was having an asthma attack. It was only later I discovered, through the local Hedgehog Group, that hedgehogs are prone to consumptive disorders.

Now then, where was I? Oh yes ... the dog has a habit of barging through the barbed wire fence which separates us from the meadow, usually when I awaken his retrieval instincts with stick, ball or rubber bone. In doing so, he inevitably leaves tufts of shoulder fur on the spikes as he goes. I can only assume that his skin is as thick as his skull because he never suffers a scratch.

I'd never regarded this hair depository as an aid to the natural world until I climbed the creaking aluminium ladder and opened the winter-damp tit box.

This year's nesting material consists of about fifty per cent delicate green moss and the rest, golden retriever cladding. The gleanings from regular dog brushing sessions are now stored in the garden shed. In the spring I'll place them strategically close to the tit box and let them help themselves.

Well, in my opinion, any dedicated parents faced with the prospect of rearing seven or eight youngsters need all the help they can get.

Great-crested Grebe

Bay Watch

The road down to Bouley Bay was deserted. The forecast had suggested the likelihood of occasional sunny intervals though it had rained persistently throughout the night.

I was heading for the beach in search of a few interesting pebbles and wet conditions are always the best when seeking out Nature's natural colours. Simple, tide-worn stones can make an intriguing ornament when gathered together and placed in water. They reflect true earth colours and, what's more, they're everlasting.

The shingle banks at Bouley Bay are by no means extensive but what they lack in size they make up for in sheer colour. Red serpentine, pleasingly laminated schist, grey and pink granite and flints. I'm no expert, but I do find this kind of beachcombing fascinating. It's just a question of time, patience and an eye for the unusual.

I worked diligently for a couple of hours then just sat, looked and listened for a while. I hadn't seen a soul since I'd been on the beach and, apart from a great-crested grebe working tirelessly among the mooring buoys, I had the bay more or less to myself.

I began timing the grebe's dives. Forty-five seconds was the longest and eight seconds the shortest. It seemed the length of time spent submerged depended largely on whether the bird caught anything.

Why I'd found myself timing the bird's endeavours I have no idea. I stored the information in the mental file marked 'Miscellaneous' and followed the flights of half-a-dozen carrion crows homing in on a point above the bay where the summer furze fire had blackened the cliff face.

Crows then began appearing from all directions and their high level conversation suggested trouble ahead. A good fifty birds all heading in the same direction usually means that someone or something was in for a bit of chivvying.

As I watched, a female marsh harrier floated into view, drifting buzzard-like over the scarred hillside. For the most part the crow crowd kept its distance but occasionally a bird crossed the tolerance line at which point the harrier would roll on her back, presenting a discouraging set of talons. I'd love to catch that amazing flying skill with a camera and play it out in slow motion.

The argument softened with distance and I crunched across the shingle towards the car, leaving a couple of rock pipits disputing the bay's ownership above the therapeutic sound of waves polishing pebbles for me.

Final Reflections

It seems like only yesterday I stood above St. Ouen's Bay on a cold, clear January morning and contemplated the contents of this journal. I wondered, at the time, whether my observations and reflections would be enough to fill its pages. Eleven months on, I find myself guilty of leaving as many holes in this Wild Island's natural story as can be found in the average prawning net. In a sense, maybe that's all to the good, because it leaves a great deal still to be said.

I very much wanted to spend time with a friend whose study of moths has produced some remarkable rarities, but the weather got in the way of the best laid plans. It had been my intention to spend more time with a camera in company with cirl buntings. Where did the time go? Filming a kingfisher which has begun to appear regularly in Nick's garden was another uncompleted project. I'm now planning to set up a hide. Filming through the double glazing leaves a lot to be desired.

However, I did manage an early morning stake-out with the local bat group which left me in no doubt that there is great merit in specialising in matters of natural history. I had imagined that it was a case of climbing into ancient barns, church steeples and cobweb-filled roof spaces but not so. There is a much more sophisticated way of separating the bat species than prying, uninvited, into their musty dormitories.

My 'batting' companions used an electronic device, complete with flashing lights, which picks up and separates the high-pitched voices of each bat species.

This may have been a brief encounter but I now know how it's possible to identify bats in the pitch dark and, as an added bonus, how to get eaten alive by midges in a predawn vigil while waiting for pipistrelles to return to roost.

My own preoccupation with birds revealed a few interesting facts. How, for instance, does a collared dove begin building a nest? At some point the first twig has to be laid in a conveniently shaped tree fork. If it's windy the twig won't stay in position by itself so one of the mating couple, and it's always hard to sex collared doves, sits on the twig. When the labouring dove returns, the bird climbs on to its partner's back, passes twig number two carefully to its mate who then tucks it carefully beneath its breast. I know this is how it's done because I actually filmed the process from my office window. A considerable number of twigs have to be bound together firmly before they can be trusted to stay in position. From the sitting bird's point of view it must be a bit like trying to make a rush mat in the dark.

The first twig

It has been an eventful and fascinating year. I've recorded it in far greater detail than those notes I'd normally jot down in a self-contrived shorthand but, even so, I've still used a very broad brush. Possibly the most important conclusion I've reached this year is that Nature's greatest vulnerability lies in the fact that to enjoy it costs nothing. Human nature, on the other hand, always demands a price tag in order to estimate what it considers true values. The danger here is in attempting to value that which is beyond price – and getting it wrong.

But enough of philosophising. The sounds of New Year celebrations are melting into the early hours of January and I can feel an irrepressible anticipation taking over from the feelings of regret at another year lost. Stretching out ahead of me through the months and seasons is yet another brand new, glorious nature trail just begging to be explored.

Happy New Year, and remember, hover-flies and dragonflies don't sting.

ABOUT THE AUTHOR AND ILLUSTRATOR

Peter Double is a Londoner by birth but Jersey has been his home since 1962. When war broke out in 1939 he was six months old and enjoying the sun on Havre des Pas beach. Evacuation from London to the Cheshire countryside during the War years provided him with an early introduction to natural history.

Time working as a chef at the Ritz in London, a period in the Merchant Navy and two years National Service preceded his decision to renew the Jersey connection and make the Island his permanent home. During the last three decades or so Peter has been involved in broadcast television, script-writing, journalism and not a little jazz clarinet playing.

Peter's favourite pursuits – bird-watching and angling – have inspired a close affinity with Jersey's natural environment. Since 1990, his involvement with a locally based video production company has given him the opportunity to master a broadcast camera; this has resulted in the production of a series of video programmes covering much of Jersey's natural habitat, fauna and flora.

Nick Parlett spent fourteen years as a graphic designer and Art Director in his home Island of Jersey, then succumbed to the lure of a new career as a wildlife artist. He first became interested in wildlife during his schooldays in the 1970s, inspired by such artists as John Gould and Sir Peter Scott, and subsequently spent much of his spare time pursuing his passion for both studying and painting wildlife.

Towards the end of the 1980s, whilst working in an office, he found himself dreaming of drawing puffins on some remote headland: "When things get that bad, it's definitely time for a change of direction and I planned to turn the dream into reality."

Two successful exhibitions in Jersey, in 1982 and '86, were encouraging, but it was not until 1991 that he finally decided to become a full-time professional wildlife artist. Keenly involved in environmental issues, Nick's work today concentrates more than ever on wildlife, both fauna and flora. His work sells widely throughout Britain and is becoming increasingly sought after. He receives a constant flow of commissions which include Jersey telephone cards and new issues of postage stamps.